The Scarlet Cord

Conversations with God's Chosen Women

For Jan,
You are such a bright light at Trinity—may God always bless your path—
Blessings,
Lindsay +

The Scarlet Cord

Conversations with God's Chosen Women

Written by

Lindsay Hardin Freeman

Paintings by

Karen Canton

BOOKS

Winchester, UK
Washington, USA

First published by O-Books, 2010
O-Books is an imprint of John Hunt Publishing Ltd., Laurel House, Station Approach, Alresford, Hants, SO24 9JH, UK
office1@o-books.net
www.o-books.com

For distributor details and how to order please visit the 'Ordering' section on our website.

ISBN: 978 1 84694 375 1

A CIP catalogue record for this book is available from the British Library.

Design: Tom Davies

Printed in the UK by CPI Antony Rowe
Printed in the USA by Offset Paperback Mfrs, Inc

CONTENTS

Endorsements

Lindsay Hardin Freeman takes us to the very heart of biblical women. Her book puts the Bible upside down for us because it has been taught by males for generations. What a refreshing perspective! Her characters are so real, breathtakingly human and intimate, not sentimental or sugar-coated. What a wonderful new way to do Bible study.
The Rev. Canon Louis (Skip) Schueddig, President, The Alliance for Christian Media and Day1, Atlanta, Georgia

Women of every faith in the Congo and Darfur, Afghanistan and Pakistan, and to a meaningful degree, everywhere on the planet, are still struggling and suffering. Thus, this re-articulation of the biblical stories — as it underscores dignity, respect and support for women — is as timely today as ever. May this insightful and heartwarming endeavor be a vigorous reminder of human potential and justice.
Barbara Forster, The Tandem Project in support of the United Nations; past Chair, Board of Directors, American Refugee Committee

Women often play key roles in scripture, but their stories are usually told from the point of view of one of the male characters. Lindsay Hardin Freeman brings twelve women to life, giving them voices of their own. We discover layers of meaning previously overlooked.
Richard H. Schmidt, Editor & Director, Forward Movement Publications

Lindsay Hardin Freeman's work is a generous and imaginative gift to her sisters!
The Rev. Mary Frances Schjonberg, Episcopal News Service National Correspondent

There's a dirty truth about theology. Almost all of it's been written by men. In The Scarlet Cord, Lindsay Hardin Freeman tells the story we male theologians have overlooked, or simply passed by. Deeply personal, intensely engaging of mind and emotion, these stories help us get inside people who grappled with God in our familiar biblical stories.
Loren B. Mead, Founder, The Alban Institute, Washington DC

An absolute and rare gem! In a book market filled with trite and feel-good spirituality, Freeman offers an engaging, pastoral and honest portrayal of biblical women that will engage and transform the hearts of both men and women. She offers a vast range of emotions including conflicting hopes, redeemed anger and transformed pain. Highly recommended.
The Very Rev. Spenser D. Simrill, Dean, St. Mark's Cathedral, Minneapolis, Minnesota

Anyone who has been disappointed (or outraged) by the one-dimensional treatment women in the Bible receive from Hollywood (or Broadway), the news media, schools and — dare I say it? — the Church, will be thrilled with Lindsay Hardin Freeman's work. Brava!
Sarah Bartenstein, Director of Communications, St. Stephen's Episcopal Church, Richmond, Virginia

This is a much needed book! All will enjoy and learn the important roles women played in Scripture, in biblical history, and in the lives of those who continue to seek God at work in the world about us. By revealing the personalities behind unique and compelling women in the Bible, The Scarlet Cord also draws out our own stories. Bravo!
The Rev. Peggy E. Tuttle, National Network of Episcopal Clergy Associations; Churches United in Christ (CUIC) Racial Justice Task Force

An important book on women and the Bible for general and devotional readers as well as serious biblical students and scholars. What truly distinguishes this book are the highly readable stories and portraits of each woman, warts-and-all, as they try to deal with life's joys and challenges in the context of faith — not unlike women today!
The Rev. Dr. Sheryl A. Kujawa-Holbrook, Professor of Religious Education, Claremont School of Theology

The Scarlet Cord is more than a collection of biblical heroine tales. It is an illuminated manuscript in the literal sense. Karen Canton's vibrant portraits paired with Lindsay Hardin Freeman's bold and lucid retellings shed light on those too

often overshadowed. This book proves that a modern woman can still look to these timeless stories to find inspiration, empowerment, and most of all, herself.
Pam Grossman, Curator, Phantasmaphile.com

What went through the mind of Rahab, the harlot, or Deborah, the warrior? And what was it like to be Mary, Jesus' mother? You will be glad to have met them anew.
A. Wayne Schwab, Director, Member Mission Network, Plattsburgh, New York

In a wonderful and powerful way, Lindsay Hardin Freeman brings to life compelling women of the Bible. No longer just characters, they are now people, with an important story to tell. Both women and men will find their understanding of the Bible enriched and deepened.
The Rev. Noel Bailey, St. Paul's Episcopal Church, Lancaster, New Hampshire

With Lindsay Hardin Freeman's riveting first-person narratives and Karen Canton's brilliant portraits, this book will inspire all God's children who seek new ways to understand Scripture — and who love a great story!
Roxanne Ezell, Calvin Presbyterian Church, Long Lake, Minnesota, and The Rev. Dr. Roger Ezell, Presbytery of the Twin Cities Area.

The Scarlet Cord — what a treat! I am excited for Karen Canton and Lindsay Hardin Freeman to see how this project has developed. It reads well and the paintings, I love. It will touch a lot of lives and I look forward to purchasing a copy for myself! Blessings
Georgia Wiester, Presbyterian Community, Buellton, California

The Scarlet Cord, a treasure trove of vivid and compelling reimaginings, gives us access to life stories that can illuminate our dark places and help us make meaning of our lives.
Barbara Braver, writer, editor, and former Assistant for Communication to Frank T. Griswold, Presiding Bishop of the Episcopal Church, Gloucester, Massachusetts

Something in my soul was awakened upon reading The Scarlet Cord. From Deborah to Mary, the courage, passion, strength and leadership showed by these women gave me inspiration and hope.
Karen Greenfeld, Roman Catholic Church of St. Gabriel, Bronx, New York

With sensitivity and flair, Lindsay Freeman offers a creative new perspective from which to view and relate to women of the Bible. Karen Canton's pictures are imaginative and simply beautiful. An inspired collaboration which I look forward to owning, savoring, and sharing.
The Rev. Canon Jean Parker Vail, Durham, North Carolina, author, *In the Name of God: Exploring God's Love in Prayer and Pulpit.*

These biblical vignettes explore womanhood by mining the familiar stories for new life-affirming insights. Canton's stunning images and Freeman's personal re-telling create a reflective pool for observing calmly the historic and defining truths of female presence in a male dominated narrative.
Mark J. Duffy, Director of Archives, The Archives of the Episcopal Church

We are able to take strength from these remarkable women who speak to us like our neighbors and friends, who reveal their doubts, their fears, their faith. In them we find examples to help us through challenges we see before us today.
Carol Barnwell, Director of Communication, Diocese of Texas

The Scarlet Cord speaks so to my heart. People in the Bible come alive as this book changes them from just "names" into real people. Magnificent reading!
Betty Zulch, St. Mark's Episcopal Church, Mount Pleasant, Texas

To the love of my life, Len, and my sons, Jeffrey and David,
all of whom bring me great joy.
Lindsay Hardin Freeman

To my husband, with love, whose untiring work made
this all possible.
Karen N. Canton

www.scarletcordbook.com

These words describe many of the women in the Bible who made history...

daring
confident
passionate
searching
spirited
defiant
focused
rebellious
stubborn
vibrant

these words generally do not...

content
complacent
charming
tranquil
polite
mild
cheerful
satisfied
obliging
amicable

Preface

These stories were compiled primarily in the early morning, when my mind was still unencumbered by the day's headlines, worries and demands. Time alone with the women in the book was really time alone with God, for they are his people first. They are people he loved, people he kindled the Holy Spirit within, people kept knocking until their questions were answered, even if the answers were different from the ones they expected, or even hoped for.

Such time with God for me was inspired by my mother, who discovered she had Hodgkin's lymphoma when I was five and she was forty-seven. Her doctors told her that she would only live for about six months. With that knowledge, each morning in our old farmhouse near Excelsior, Minnesota, she would kneel by a bed in an upstairs room and pray for about twenty minutes. I picture her now. The few times I interrupted her, she was clearly in conversation, albeit silent. Pain was on her face and no doubt in her body. But she was not by herself; that I could tell. There was Someone else there. It was a holy space and she was not alone.

She did not talk about the cancer with me, nor her impending death. In those days, it was thought that children could not handle such details. Now I realize, through years of trying to reconcile her action of silence with my need to grieve and say goodbye, that we were her last refuge, her place of safety — and she, in fact, could not bring herself to say goodbye to us.

She lived six more years. During that time, she found the strength both to live and then to die, leaving her beloved family safe in God's hands. She seemed surprisingly happy during those years, and I believe that joy was due to both God's healing grace and being able to let go through prayer.

Women, like my mother and like the women here, live with

thoughts and passions that are not necessarily revealed to the world, or even to the ones they love. This book, through first-person narrative, enters into that personal space of intense privacy.

When we are gathered around God's table one day, packed in that big room with many others, I will be delighted to see the woman who confronted Jesus by the well, to finally understand what caused Eve to step away from the One who made her, and to see if Mary, Jesus' mother, is all she is cracked up to be. She must be.

They are with me now. Throughout the ages, their actions and personalities have inspired God's followers and those who search for spiritual truth.

And they are not alone in the Communion of Saints, for all those whom we love and who have loved God are there, the tears wiped from their faces and all sense of time rolled into God's time.

I wish for you the deep sense of self and God that my mother knew, particularly in those early morning hours. I wish for you the passion these twelve women had, passion that filled their lives, inspired their children — and changed the human race.

Lindsay Hardin Freeman

Introduction

Rahab, the woman pictured on the front of this book, was a prostitute. She also happens to be a great-grandmother (many times over) of King David and a direct ancestor of Jesus. How did she get in the Bible, much less in such royal company? A quick answer: She helped tens of thousands of Israelites complete their journey from slavery to freedom, joining the roster of many noble souls who shared in building the foundation of the Judeo-Christian tradition.

Check her hands. They hold a scarlet cord, which she hung out her window to make sure the spies she sheltered would save her, for Jericho itself and its residents – young and old, male and female, human and animal – would soon be annihilated. And then look at the other women in this book. A scarlet cord appears in every painting, linking them together, for they all faced challenges, sometimes seemingly insurmountable, and took actions that have marked both their lives and the Judeo-Christian story.

Although most made great sacrifices and acted out of love, their deeds were not always selfless; their decisions were not always made for the greater good. One munched the forbidden fruit; another simply wanted to find the one she loved. One gave birth to Jesus; still another bestowed upon him profound comfort, anointing him six days before his death. They all pushed the boundaries – cultural, emotional and sexual – and they all contributed toward where we, as God's people, find ourselves today.

And if they had said no?

What would the world be like if the women in this book had said no when God called them forth? What would have happened if Mary had rebuffed the angel Gabriel? What if there was no one to meet Jesus at the tomb after he had been raised from the dead? What if the women who risked their safety on that predawn walk to Jesus' tomb had stayed away out of fear, as the disciples did? And what if Eve had not taken the apple, setting humankind on a course toward both knowledge and sin? That old Garden might be getting a little crowded by now.

Not only would the course of biblical history be changed, but human history as well. Yet the deeds of many of these twelve women, and the other named women mentioned in the Bible (there are less than two hundred) have most often gone unnoticed. Shedding light on that dark corner of history and theology, this book explores — through dialogue, choice and action — the lives of twelve courageous Bible women. Smaller insets of female contemporaries also accompany the text in several chapters.

White fire

How best to read these stories, to assimilate the art? Jewish tradition uses a dynamic tool for interpreting the Bible: black fire and white fire. The words themselves are the black fire: writings handed down from generation to generation. White fire is the space between the words, the place where readers use imagination, intellect, creativity and personal experience to better understand each story.

Through word and art, this book uses both black and white fire. Journalistic queries — what, where, when, why and how — have been researched, checking both Jewish and Christian sources and multiple Bible translations. Black fire was studied and white fire was kindled, filling in such blanks as: What did Ruth and Naomi eat on their journey from Moab to Bethlehem? What might Mary Magdalene have felt after her long grief-filled walk to Jesus' tomb, only to find it empty? How could Eve have possibly believed the serpent enough to change forever her relationship with God? Deeper fictional details were added in several places, particularly during Eve's walk to the Tree of Knowledge, in the encounter between King Solomon and the women from *The Song of Songs*, and in Mary's story about her life following the death of Jesus.

That same imagination has been applied with each brush stroke of the artist, incorporating both ancient and contemporary motifs. Look carefully at each painting, for the artist has captured the spirit of each woman, offering symbols that help personalize the hallmarks of her story. The scarlet cord in each painting reminds us that these women are linked through such character assets as faith, courage and the willingness to act. They are all part of a larger story — God's story — and are not appendages, unworthy of the recognition that men in Scripture have received through the ages.

Friends around a campfire

The Hebrew Bible, known as the Old Testament to most Christians, forms the foundation for telling the Christian story. In this retelling of classic stories from both the Old and New Testaments, several of the earliest women speak as if they are looking across the ages, while, in their lifetimes of course, they did not know about Jesus. These women, and all others who took part in God's unfolding plans throughout the centuries are part of what the Anglican tradition refers to as the Communion of Saints. For now, think of them as friends around a campfire, sharing intimate memories and moments of their lives.

God's story would not have been the same

Each woman in this book — and there are murderers and homemakers, warriors and mothers — was confronted with a particular dilemma and responded from the heart, full of courage. There are no shrinking violets here. Whatever their particular contribution, God's story would not have been the same had they failed to act. And let me take a theological risk here. Many scholars believe that God does not need humans to be complete; I disagree. God's story is not complete without ours. We are part of the greatest story ever told, the biblical story. Even though the canon of the Bible may be complete, the story of God's people is unfinished. Actions still matter. Relationships count. Like these women in years past, decisions made today will influence those who live tomorrow, as well as those who live thousands of years from now.

It is the reader who will absorb the individual meaning from each story, assimilate it with her or his own experience, and then choose, or not, to turn that story into action. Perhaps a reader experiencing infertility will choose to lay more of her burden at God's feet, much like Hannah. Maybe a soldier on the battlefield will ask God to walk beside her, as Deborah did, and be guided into life-changing decisions, for her and for her enemies. Or perhaps, like Rahab, a reader who has become trapped in a life of dead ends will find the courage to break free.

I hope that all of us, standing at the empty tomb with Mary Magdalene and witnessing the astonishing presence of the risen Christ, will never be the same. May we know that we are part of God's story, that we too have our own parts to play, and that our actions matter, forever.

There is no question in my mind that these women existed, that they took actions that changed the course of their lives and their faith, and that they helped build the foundation of both the Jewish and Christian traditions. May their stories continue to give us both strength and joy.

<table>
<tr>
<td>

Rahab:

- Decisive
- Bold
- Spontaneous
- Protective
- Sensual
- Faithful

</td>
<td>

Text: *Joshua 2, 6*

Setting: *Jericho, about 1250 BC*[1]

Significance: *At great risk to herself, a prostitute named Rahab provides shelter for two Hebrew spies and enables the fledgling Jewish nation to gain entrance to the Promised Land.*

</td>
</tr>
</table>

Chapter 1

Rahab: From Harlot to Hero

From my roof I heard the strong, urgent knock. I'll tell you this: I was in no hurry to answer it. It had been a busy week and my roof is my blessing place where I go and not worry, not talk, not shut down emotionally.

I do some weaving; it's there I keep my bundles of flax. From my roof I study the skies. Late at night the stars loom so brightly that I feel I am a part of something bigger than myself. And then I am whole. Different from downstairs.

Some call me a harlot, others a prostitute. Does it matter? I did what I had to do in the ancient walled city of Jericho to survive. As a young girl I had been taken into the king's harem, one of many virgins seemingly plucked off the streets at random to please a powerful, if aging, monarch. Thank God I had never had children. When he finally died, I ran away rather than be raped by his brutal son, for all the harem went to the first in line for the throne. Of course no one would call it rape but me.

It was only because I had made friends with the king's guards that I wasn't killed, for doing so was treason. They were the ones who let me live, who somehow worked a deal with the son. By all rights, I should be dead, but I volunteered to act as a spy for the king,[2] feeding word back to the guards of any stranger trying to make his way into Jericho. My family wouldn't have me back, for they believed I had disgraced them. I turned to the only thing I could do: selling myself.

And if I hadn't been in that business, God's people might not have made it out of the wilderness alive.

Knock. Knock. Getting louder.

I stuck my head through a hole in the wall and looked down.

From my house, built right into the twelve-story wall that surrounded our city, I could see two men. One kept glancing around, nervous, worried. The other was up and down off the step like he had either a woman or the law on his trail. I'm used to that; men are often eager to get into my house without being seen.

Knock. Knock. Stronger, urgent.

"All right, all right, I'm coming!" I called, smoothing my hair back and straightening my shoulders. I have given up some things to survive, but never my pride. Or my looks, for that matter.

✠

The men were rugged and tan. One was young and handsome with deep-set eyes; the other, while weather-beaten, carried his shoulders in such a way that I could have tied two planks across them. Often men I see are a bit sallow, with better days gone by. These two were different.

"Please, let us in," said Deep Eyes. "Now."

"Yes?" I said, holding my head high.

"One night, maybe two," said the older one, hurriedly. The younger one studied me; I knew what he was thinking.

They spoke with accents, still anxious. One kept turning to look behind him. They were here for a reason, like all men.

Suddenly I knew who they were. They were from the rebel army camped on the other side of the Jordan River, east of town, over the hills. They had been massing there for several weeks. We knew they wanted our town. They weren't the first warriors to come along; that's why our city had the walls it did.

Travelers had told stories of these people, the Hebrews, for years. They had leveled over sixty towns between us and Egypt, killing men and women, burning entire villages, kidnapping young girls and keeping them as captives. If they felt like letting them live.

What's more, some said they had magic. We had heard that their God had split the Red Sea for them so they could flee the Egyptians. Plagues had befallen those who kept them in slavery. Bread had dropped from the sky so they wouldn't starve. When they thirsted in the desert, water had gushed from rocks at God's command.

Would they kill me? If I screamed, maybe someone would hear me. But most likely not. After all, my feelings aren't exactly the town's top priority.

Faith or no faith.

All those years I had wondered if their God was more than magic. I could use some of that protection myself. Lately I had even begun to pray, hoping that my voice would be heard.

Faith or no faith.

"Stay," I said, my voice suddenly sounding high pitched. "Stay. You will be safe here."

Money deserves privacy, so I bolted the door behind them.

✠

I won't tell you all the details of that late afternoon but I will tell you that there was something about the younger one that worked my stomach over. He was surprisingly kind. That does not happen often in this business. I can't wait on kindness or I'd be out of work. Like my friend down the street who has to beg for food and sleeps wedged into the wall.

I listened to their talk as the sun beat down on the house, making all in its path slow like thirsty camels.

"These people don't look so big," said the older one, continuing his watch out the second-floor window.

"You're right," said Deep Eyes. "Forty years ago we never made it because everyone got scared. They said we were like grasshoppers among giants. Maybe we were. Not anymore."

Then he turned to me.

"Rahab," he said, actually having learned my name, "God means for us to have this land. He promised it to us. We will have it peacefully or we will take it violently. But we will have it — and with more descendants than there are stars in the sky."

✠

I thought of that sky, of the stars coming to life over my roof. There was more to life than what appeared on the grimy streets below. Sometimes I even thought of the stars as my children, for they were as close to offspring as I would ever see. Was it possible that Someone was setting those stars in motion, separating light from dark, order from chaos?

Suddenly something wasn't right; I could see the older man strain to see down the street as we heard loud voices. Shouting, ugly, urgent voices. Coming toward my house. Then knocking, loud knocking with booming, shattering break-the-house-down kind of blows to my heavy wooden front door.

"We have a message from the King!" came the voices from the street. "Send out the men who are in your house! They are spies getting ready to attack the city!"

Flashing before me were my nights on the roof. Was their God real? Would their God save me, too?

"They will kill us all! Open this door NOW!"

Within seconds, all became clear to me.

I rushed the men up a floor to the roof where they burrowed like moles under stalks of flax I had drying there, piled high. Knowing I would be killed if found hiding our enemies, I tried to restart my breathing as I flew back down the stairs.

"Let us in! Let us in! We know they're in there!"

Opening the door, I smiled, lifting my chin. Years of practice had taught me well as I caught the eye of one of the guards I had known. Intimately.

"The men you are looking for are not here! They're gone,

headed that way," I said, pointing toward the hills outside the city.

"You can catch them if you hurry. They are no more spies than your grandmothers are."

The guard caught my look, turned, and raced toward the city gates, the others on his heels.

I shut and bolted the door. That was close. But my life was still in danger.

Hurriedly I ran up the stairs.

"Listen," I whispered, "I've seen too much not to believe that God wants you to have this land, and that he indeed is the God of the heavens above and the earth below.

"I guarded you today with my own life. Now I demand you do the same for me. Swear to me that you will protect me, my mother, my father, my brothers and my sisters when you invade."

My family? Was that me talking? Why save them? They had shunned me.

Apparently I still cared, more than I knew.

I drew taller and waited for their reply. They were still wanted men and all I had to do was scream.

No answer. Grabbing my throat, I started to yell.

"All right, Rahab!" said the older one, clamping down on my shoulders. "Our lives for yours. We will keep you and your family safe. Make sure your whole family is here, not on the streets, not away from this house."

"Behold, when we come into the land, you shall bind this scarlet cord in the window through which you let us down, and you shall gather into your house your father and mother, your brothers, and all your father's household." Joshua 2:19

"And here," said Deep Eyes, fishing from his pack, "hang this scarlet cord from the window to remind us that this is where you live."

When all was dark and finally quiet, I let the men down on a rope from my window, right over the outer city wall. "Hide in the hill country for three days until they are no longer looking for you," I said, my breathing almost back to normal.

Late that night, after gathering the few in my family who believed me, I hung the cord from the window, hoping it wouldn't draw too much attention.

Nights found me asleep beside it, grasping what seemed like a magical connection. Only I so hoped it wasn't.

"Have I not commanded you? Be strong and of good courage; be not frightened, neither be dismayed; for the Lord your God is with you wherever you go." Joshua 1:9

For the first time, I found myself praying.

God, if you are there, keep me safe. I need something stronger than me for a change.

We waited for three long weeks, only running out for food and water. To pass the time, I thought of other stories I had heard, like how the Hebrew people had lived in slavery for hundreds of years, desperately wanting to be free of Egyptian tyranny and cruelty.

Moses had demanded, on behalf of God, that Pharaoh let his people go. Nothing changed, though, even after God caused plague after plague to get his attention: rivers running red with blood, frogs overtaking the Nile, cattle dying from boils and other diseases. Still, nothing.

Finally, God told the people to splash lamb blood over their front doors. Then he sent his angel of death to kill the firstborn Egyptian sons. The angel saw the blood and spared each Hebrew boy. The Israelites, their children safe, left the land, finally free.

Would God save me, too? To most, I was nothing but a whore who lured husbands and sons into my bed. Did God see me as someone more? Or did I deserve the sword like everyone else?

I fingered my scarlet cord. Carefully I moved it a few inches closer to the door in case that angel of death came by. Maybe the color would provoke some long ago memories of letting at least a few people live.

These people had a powerful God. But as far as I could see, once you were in, you were in. I wanted in. I held the cord tighter and prayed.

God, you have kept me alive this far. If there is any chance I might be saved, please spare me. Use me for your purposes, all that I am. Don't leave me here to die.

✠

Several weeks later a blast rang through the town. Thousands of soldiers fell behind their leader as the priests blew trumpets. For six days they marched around Jericho, no words spoken, all attention on the trumpets.

Joshua, fit the battle of Jericho, Jericho, Jericho
Joshua, fit the battle of Jericho
And the walls come tumbling down
African-American spiritual

The noise was loud; on the seventh day, it was deafening. Seven times the Israelite soldiers advanced behind the trumpets, their faces grim. As one last explosive blast echoed through the land, they screamed as loudly as they could. Then, bloody mayhem. It wasn't just a case of the wall falling, I'll tell you that. These Hebrews were warriors. All of what I knew crumbled around me. I could hear the desperate cries of neighbors, then silence. The scream from my friend who slept wedged in the wall is something I will never forget.

But we were safe. The Hebrews looked for the scarlet cord, rescued us, and we fled Jericho with them. Imagine that. Saving a prostitute and killing the others.

Those stars I used to look at, wondering if I was part of something bigger than myself? The spies had been right. Their people did have as many descendants as there were stars in the sky.

I should know, for I married Deep Eyes and his people's faith became my own.

Four generations later, my great-grandson David was born. He became the greatest king of Israel. Am I using the word "great" too much there? Blame it on love. And pride. Those bright stars in the sky that I used to pretend were my children suddenly were.

And almost 1100 years later, Jesus came along. He's my direct descendant, too, which is quite something. Deep in his lineage, he has someone who's a little different: Me.

The way I look at it, Jesus and I were both rebels. Rebels who wanted something more, rebels who believed in something more, rebels of the heart.

Why does Rahab matter today?

Passionate and bold, courageous and decisive, Rahab believed in herself and had an emerging faith in God. The lowest of the low — an outsider to the faith and a prostitute — she risked her own life to bring freedom to God's people. God did not forget her; indeed, he honored her by helping her escape prostitution, find a family, and be an ancestor of Jesus. Through her actions, Rahab reminds us to believe in ourselves and to have faith, for we are all valuable to God. She also reminds us that there are no "perfect" Christians. God will always seek the best from us — and often surprises us by whom he chooses for important missions.

"By faith Rahab the harlot did not perish with those who were disobedient, because she had given friendly welcome to the spies."
Hebrews 11:31

What learnings might Rahab inspire?

- Although it would appear that Rahab made a spot decision that turned her life toward God, clearly she — and God — had been working toward that moment. Have you ever faced such a juncture? What was your response and how did it make a difference? What have you learned about God since?

- Rahab was a rather dynamic addition to Jesus' family tree. Theologically and practically, what does that mean? How might it make Jesus more accessible to all? To you?
- What was it Rahab had been searching for before the spies came to her door? How would that have influenced her decision? How might God have been present in her life before her bold decision? What are decisions that you are facing now in which God might be making his presence known?
- Although Rahab was a prostitute, she was able to use her life in God's service. She found redemption. What are some aspects of your life, that while not as perfect as you would like, might be used to further God's work in the world?

To learn more about Rahab, see page 163.

Eve:

- Restless
- Unsatisfied
- Autonomous
- Gullible
- Searching
- Defiant

Text: *Genesis 3,4*

Setting: *The Garden of Eden,*

Significance: *By eating the forbidden fruit and encouraging Adam to eat it as well, Eve incites God's anger, and they are ejected from the Garden.*

Chapter 2

Eve: Just a Bite, You'll Like It

We had built none of Eden
but it was beautiful
the animals
the land
the food
all was well
but maybe that was the problem
it was all God's
so when the serpent asked
again that morning
I finally stopped.
    Eve,
    is this enough?
    you're happy
    you're content
    complacent
    but don't you want more?
    passion
    fire
    life
    God wants more from you too
she tilted her head
toward It
No, serpent, no.
God told us that we may know everything
we may touch everything
we may have everything
except that fruit

I know, Eve
I know
she was not wicked then
she was the most beautiful
creature in the garden
golden hued feathers
long wisps of curled tail
wings of rounded sheen
eyes deep and calling forth
I trusted her
she was my friend
so I looked again
how can knowledge be bad, Eve?
you're your own person
how can one taste change all that?
besides, he loves you
he must not want you to grow up
he must not think you are ready
to know more
to be more
that must be it
she held it out
touch-me red
glistening with dew
no blemishes on it
nor on me
take it, Eve
just a bite
you'll like it
it'll be our secret
trust me
and with that she waited
silence
silence

silence
it seemed
I could not move
feet mired in muck
but was I not an adult?
do not adults make their own choices?
is that not part of growing up?
I wanted it
so I ate
juicy for a minute
sweet for a time
but I have almost forgotten
the taste
we lost our home that day
one of many points of pain
God's trust was gone
thankfully his love was not
It hurt
still does

the throes of childbirth
just the start
one of my sons
killed the other
Adam is bone tired
but what if we had stayed?
always birds in the nest
forever suckling at the breast
endlessly spoon-fed
I chose the fruit
I bear the scars
the world bears the pain
growing up is not easy
I AM.

Eve

How many times can a heart break? Why is that over hundreds of years, the pain of losing my sons has never gone away? I so wish for numbness at best, but God has never granted peace, only agony, since that horrible day.

Did I bring this pain on myself? Perhaps. Yes, I suppose I did.

Now the serpent was more crafty than any other wild animal that the LORD God had made. Genesis 3:1

You know the story. God didn't want us to eat the apple. But I ate it. I had been eyeing that tree most of my life, knowing it was the only thing out of reach. The serpent had been my friend, egging me on, year after year, season after season.

We would walk together late in the day, when Adam was out strolling with God. They had their alone time; we had ours. The serpent would only come out when God was preoccupied. Otherwise, I didn't see her and looked forward to our moments together.

That's right. The serpent was a "she." Or so I thought. Is that so strange?

I yearned for female companionship, and the serpent found that weakness. She seemed to understand things that Adam didn't. Don't get me wrong. Adam and I were flesh of one flesh, bone of one bone, heart of one heart.

But the serpent was my friend.

She would ask questions and nod her head. She listened. She had the ability that no other creature in the garden had — she could change her appearance on a whim.

Some afternoons she looked like a beautiful bird, and I would run my hand over her glistening feathers. Several times she appeared as a bounding lion; my heart lurched into my throat before my screams turned to laughter.

Other days she would emerge as a gazelle, and amaze me with her graceful speed. For several seasons, she appeared as a woman, walking beside me, step by step, convincing me just by her countenance that I wasn't alone. Those were my best days. I had never seen another woman before. No longer was I isolated with thoughts Adam did not understand.

One thing never changed, despite her transformed appearances — her eyes. They were always a deep green, a knowing and vibrant green. It seemed as though nothing bad could come from one whose eyes were so alive.

How wrong I was. How horribly wrong I was.

Like her appearance, our conversations ran the gamut, except that we always seemed to come back to one topic: the apple. She was particularly interested in it. So was I.

"Why don't you just eat it, Eve?"

"You know that God said not to."

"He doesn't mean it."

"You're wrong. I think he does."

"Just eat it. You've always wanted it."

"I can't."

✠

One day, strolling beside me as a sleek lion, she tried a new twist.

"Maybe he said no because he really meant yes. He knows you love him, Eve. If you eat the apple, you'll be more like him, not less. That would be good, right? So if he said 'don't eat it,' maybe he meant 'yes, eat it!'"

What was the logic of that?

I shook my head, as always, but she pressed on.

"He's got Adam out there every day. He's leaving you alone with the apple. Maybe he's doing that on purpose. Maybe he knows it's something you need."

Day after day, season after season, her words wore me down. I was getting worn down in other ways too. One day I found myself bored, listless. I wanted more, but didn't even know what that "more" was.

She arrived as a woman that day. Somehow she had figured out that the apple was not the only thing ripe for the plucking.

We strolled, as usual. We talked, as usual, as only the two of us could, our conversation meandering, but our feet surprisingly deliberate. Somehow I was not surprised when we stopped before the object of so many of our conversations. Like a glorious sunset profiling color combinations that drew me in as a moth to light, the tree held out its fruit like offerings, delicacies.

She reached up. Casually. Easily. I would have thought she'd have taken her time. Acted a bit scared, perhaps, a bit hesitant.

And then she picked that thing off like a greedy squirrel chases down an acorn, rolling it out in her long beautiful fingers for me.

I stood transfixed. The apple, taken from the straightest and longest branch, glimmered in the late afternoon light. It was the most beautiful thing I had ever seen, every tiny bit of it flawless. No bruises. No worms. No dips or dents.

How could God not want me to have it?

It seemed the most perfect thing I had ever known.

"Go ahead, Eve. Just a bite. You will become wise. More like God, knowing about both good and evil. He won't even know. It'll be our secret."

On that blackest of all days, heaven knows why, I listened. I could walk away no longer. I reached for it and took a bite.

So when the woman saw that the tree was good for food, and that it was a delight to the eyes, and that the tree was desired to make one wise, she took of its fruit and ate... Genesis 3:6a

✠

Juice was dribbling down my chin a few minutes later when Adam found me. Somehow the woman had disappeared, but I had barely noticed, drunk with my newfound power.

"Go ahead," I said, waving my arms and legs in a little shuffle as I held up the crisp forbidden fruit. "Have a taste! Look at me. I'm fine. She was right! Maybe God really did want us to have it!"

I placed the apple in Adam's palm.

"No, Eve," he said, his face turning pale, his hand trembling. "No."

"Go ahead," I said, the words of the woman seeming to magically appear from my lips. "Just eat it. Besides, God isn't here. He won't know. You don't want me to do this by myself, do you?"

Although his mouth said one thing, his hand said another. Holding the apple by his side, he ran his fingers over it gently, probing, almost as if to see if it was real.

All seemed silent in that moment. The whole garden seemed to watch, holding its breath.

His eyes met mine. "I'm with you, Eve," he said. "I'm with you."

My beloved raised the forbidden fruit to his lips.

If I was going down the wrong road, he would be right beside me.

Strangely enough, I loved him more in that moment than I think I ever had. Seconds later, though, my heart broke as he halfheartedly crunched the tangy fruit.

Tears came to his eyes as he spit it out and threw the core into the bushes. He stalked off without a word, only to show up hours later, infuriated.

✠

It was then we heard the rustle that for years had brought us joy. God was out in the garden, looking for us.

Suddenly aware we had no clothes, we ran behind a sparkling rock formation.

"Where are you?" God called.

"We heard you, so we hid," Adam answered, shivering. It wasn't the cold, for the temperature was always perfect in the garden.

"Who told you that you were naked?"

Then the words that I would forever hear, ringing in my ears.

"Have you eaten the fruit that I commanded you not to eat?"

It's over. It's over.

"Yes," answered Adam, "but it was the woman you gave me who brought me the fruit, and I ate it."

The man said, "The woman whom you gave to be with me, she gave me fruit from the tree, and I ate.
Genesis 3:12

The woman you gave me? Even in my fear I heard those words, clear as a bell. *The woman you gave me. Thanks, Adam.*

"How could you do such a thing? I gave you all you needed. I gave you a beautiful home, a place where all you had to do was enjoy it."

"The serpent tricked me," I croaked. "She is my friend and she gave it to me and I ate it."

The serpent tricked me. Is that the best I could do?

"Your friend indeed," he said. "Your friend indeed."

The woman said, "The serpent beguiled me, and I ate."
Genesis 13b

God strode over to a stand of ever-blossoming lilac bushes and walloped the center bush with his right foot.

"Out with you!" he commanded. "Out!"

Cowering, a bruised serpent face peeked from behind the bushes.

"Your friend was never your friend," God said. "Your friend is your enemy, and will slither on the ground the rest of her days for what she has done to you."

Scales replaced smooth beautiful skin as her muscled and taut body turned into that of an oily black snake. Clumps of greasy hair lay matted on the ground. No longer were her eyes the compelling green I had so loved; they had changed into a shade as black as a night without stars. Once the source of smooth and comforting words, her now-forked tongue could only flick. For once, though, I was not the center of her attention. It had never been about me.

She was in a standoff, albeit mute, with God. Her head and trunk rose off the ground, her body doing a strange alternating dance of impotence and violence.

"Enough!" said God. "Be gone, Satan!"

✠

She glanced at me as she slid away, but it was not with fear or affection or even regret. In that moment, as her newly hooded eyes found me, I saw something I did not expect: triumph.

Suddenly I understood.

All the other facades had been disguises, crafted to match my moods, not hers. I had been betrayed, day after day after day. I had trusted one who wanted nothing good for me. I had given my soul away to one who wanted no more than to crush it and leave it trampled on the ground for God to find. Just like he had.

It was all so obvious now.

How could I have been so wrong?

God looked at my beloved, the one from whom I had sprung, flesh from flesh, bone from bone.

"Adam, you ate the apple, just like Eve. You will be punished. From now until you return to the ground as dust, you will work and toil and sweat to provide for your family. You won't have an easy time of it. You will scrabble and fail and rise again and again to force growth from the land because I am cursing it. Otherwise, you will starve. Eve did not force you to eat the apple. You took it on your own."

Fear gripped the muscles in my legs and my knees gave way.

Never sick before, I was now violently ill. I didn't talk to God that often, and now I was throwing up in his face.

"I know you wanted to grow up, Eve," said God. "I trusted you. Adam wanted to be with me, but you needed more freedom. I knew you were flirting with evil — daily — but I wasn't going to lead you every step of the way, even here. You still had choices.

"But you chose to listen to one who misled you.

"Eve, because of your actions, you will have immense pain in childbirth. You will produce children in agony, with blood and sweat and tears. And Adam will rule."

Children? What was he talking about? Animals produced children, not us. Blood and tears in giving birth? No. No. No, to all of it!

"Now you must go, for your own sake and for Adam's. This is no longer your home. Go. Now."

With that, we were turned out of the only home we had ever known. The green of the garden seemed to evaporate behind us. Desert sand, burning desert sand, covered everywhere we looked. God was right. He had cursed the ground.

A cherub appeared at our backs, apparently stationed by God to keep us away. I had seen angels before, dancing, cavorting, flying, but this was no kind angel, no playful one. Ironically, he appeared to be half human and half lion as he guarded the entrance to our old home with a thunderous, menacing attitude. A flaming sword beside him rotated, further barring us.

Were we that evil? Adam wasn't. Was I? Was I so bad that I had to be fenced out? Would God's emissary harm us should we turn back? I thought for a minute about charging the gate — for a cherub is not dangerous — but the sword changed my mind. Would God have me impaled if I tried?

I decided against it.

Shivering and hungry — the last thing I'd eaten was that damn apple — with no idea where to find food, we fled into the suddenly cold night, running into an isolated stand of olive trees.

Once there, feelings rose within us, both new and violent. Passion. Fear. Anger. Yearning.

We had embraced before, of course, but that night was different. That night, and in the nights and years to come, we made love with a new ferocity.

I had known that God had taken Adam's rib to make me; the scar on his chest still showed. So when we came together in love, I found it to be a place I had always belonged. Despite our actions, we were one. Not just in mind and heart, but in body and soul.

✠

The garden had been God's paradise, and ours as well. This strange land, though, this new life, was hard, brutal work. Rather than basking in the afternoon light at the end of every day with God, Adam would fall asleep, exhausted. His back became crippled over the hundreds of years that God gave us to live, his hands blackened by turning burning desert sand into dirt with what he scratched and carried from the roots of the few growing plants and trees.

But there, on that cursed ground, in that burning hot sun by day and cold desert air by night, the greatest miracle of all occurred — our sons.

God thought he punished me through the pain of childbirth. Maybe he did. But I would give anything to feel that agony right now. Because with that pain came joy, tears, a new soul, a suckling mouth at the breast, cries in the night, a reason to get up. Life.

Day after day I think of my boys, Cain and Abel, they of the lanky legs and burnished faces. I think of the joy they brought me in those early years when all seemed lost. I taught them language and love; Adam showed them how to provide food and shelter. Even as a boy, first-born Cain became a master agrarian, finding the seeds of wild plants carried from the garden by birds, and raising them into rows of neatly tilled and thriving crops.

Abel had a knack with the animals. In the garden they hadn't needed training, for they were tame. Lions would lie down with lambs. Egrets would nuzzle against cougars. Turtles would challenge hares to races and leave us laughing hysterically at the results. We wouldn't eat any of them, of course; they were our friends. After all, there were ripe hanging fruits and succulent vegetables year round. That was then.

✠

Outside the garden, the animals turned on one another and on us. On several occasions, we were attacked — once by a lion, then by a boar, and another time by a meerkat. Adam had named the ancestors of these creatures, so it was heartbreaking for him to slay those whom God had designed to be our companions.

Like them, though, we had to eat. We would not let our young die for lack of courage or food. It was with Abel that Adam found a companion in hunting and fishing. The two of them would go off for days, always returning with an animal that would keep us fed and clothed.

When he was not hunting, Abel learned to raise animals for our use — lambs, goats and fowl. We would never know the peace of the garden again and its non-killing ways, but survival was the goal.

So it went on, season after season, year after year. Age and death seemed irrelevant. There was no thought of us dying. We knew of death, of course; we saw it regularly, we seemed immune to it. Or so I thought.

Perhaps it was the quiet that tipped us off. The almost deadly quiet.

Usually in the late afternoon birds sung as the shadows deepened. We had planned a favorite meal that night — roasted lamb with fresh greens. Adam and I waited, near our favorite spot, a lookout overlooking a ravine on the Tigris River.

Cain was to bring the greens and Abel, the meat. It was a celebration, for earlier in the day the boys had presented God with the fruits of their toil, the best of the harvest.

Abel had chosen the youngest and most perfect of his lambs with which to honor God. Cain had selected fruits and vegetables without blemish.

We waited. And waited. Strangely enough, there were no birds calling, no early crickets breaking the silence.

Then I saw it. A large dead tree down the hillside from me held dozens of turkey vultures. Were they sleeping? Awake?

Three vultures circled the sky. Up and down. Large arcs, then small. Smaller and smaller became the circles until the ugly birds dove for something crumpled on the ground. Other vultures in the tree readied themselves for flight, their wings spread while still hovering on the branches.

Something. Crumpled.

From where I stood I could see a mix of brown and blue and red. It was the size of a man, although I knew it to be an animal.

Men don't die, so there was nothing to worry about.

Perhaps it was a deer, or a caribou. An elk. It must be an elk, as they had been foraging through the river bottom en masse lately.

Men don't die.

My legs took off as if they were disconnected from my heart, with Adam charging behind me.

As we slid down the river embankment, I could almost hear the long-ago shouts of my boys as they shrieked with joy, plunging down the muddy hillside into the cool and pure water.

There were no such sounds today. Just silence.

Suddenly the brown and blue mass took shape.

"NOOOOOOOOOOOOOOO!" I screamed.

"NOOOOOOOOOOOOOOO!"

The lifeless body of Abel lay bludgeoned at my feet. My son, my beloved second born, the one so full of life and laughter, a boy who had brought us so much joy after we had finally scraped our lives together, lay dead.

I pulled him to my chest, cradling, rocking, clutching. Adam, ashen-faced, threw his arms around both of us as if to protect us from unseen forces that had killed our beloved boy. It seemed like hours as we lay there grieving. It could get no worse than this.

But somehow it did.

We were not alone.

Cain emerged from the shadows, bruised and marked. He looked to have a burn on his forehead while the rest of his face was as white as ash.

He stood silent. And then I knew. The way he glanced away, the way he could not hold my look reminded me of that horrible snake in the garden so many years ago.

"Don't you think I loved my brother? Do you think I wanted this to happen?

It was now my turn for silence. I couldn't speak even if I wanted to.

The buzzards remained poised on the tree limbs, watching us sort out death from life, love from hate.

"What is that mark on your head?" Adam asked.

"God put it there to protect me."

"Why should God protect you? What have you done?"

Then the words came, the words that would leave my heart forever splintered.

"I killed Abel," he said. "I killed my brother."

My bones felt torn apart, wrenched one by one from my torso.

Don't tell me that you did this!

"You...you...killed him? You KILLED him? WHY?"

The Lord said to Cain, "Where is Abel your brother?" He said, "I do not know; am I my brother's keeper?" And the Lord said, "What have you done? The voice of your brother's blood is crying to me from the ground." Genesis 4:9-10

"God cursed the food I brought," he said. "He would not accept that I was turning this cursed ground into something good. God wanted the animals. Abel brought seven of his best, and I brought what I grew. God took the animals, but not what I brought."

I was still in a stupor.

"You killed your brother," I said. "You killed your brother."

Cain looked at me one more time before he turned his back and left forever. We never heard from him again, although I heard he settled in the land of Nod.

✠

I lost both my sons that day. There are some things that parents never get used to, and losing a child tops the list. Some of my pain has worn away over time, but never all.

If I had never eaten the apple, would all of this have happened? Would my boys still be alive?

I wish that I could say I forgave myself, but I did not. If I had left the apple alone, we would still be in the garden. Abel would not be dead and Cain would not be gone.

But perhaps I would never even have had sons. They were born outside the garden, not in. Then I wonder again: Why was the apple off limits? What was the serpent doing in the garden? Did God mean for us to have children but not there? Why?

There is much I don't know.

If was as if God wanted to keep us young. Children, while often blessed, are never really on their own. Adam and I grew up *outside* the walls of the garden; it never happened inside.

While the apple was without bruises, I am full of them. That apple, though, was a tool. A tool for God and bait for the Evil One. Unlike the apple, I stand on my own now, with no owner but myself.

God gave us the ability to question, to act on our own, to discern, to use our own minds and our own spirits. I thank God for the ability to trip and fall and get up again — and yes, to love.

Why does Eve matter today?

Determined and resolute, inquisitive and rebellious, Eve will forever be linked to that first step away from God, the first sin. She is also the first woman — and like the rest of us, she is full of both strengths and weaknesses. She was tempted, she sinned, and yet she carried on. She knew pain and agony, but she persevered. Life can be cruel and hard due to our choices, but as Eve also discovered, God will never abandon us.

What learnings might Eve inspire?

- Eve's taking of the fruit symbolizes the human race turning away from God. Does her struggle remind you of similar moments in your life? If so, how has God maintained a relationship with you? What has been your response?
- The Book of Genesis (3:1) identifies the serpent as the "most crafty figure in the garden." History has always assumed the male voice for the great tempter, but who is to say what form or gender it took? One thing is sure: like a child molester, the serpent would have presented itself as trustworthy, reliable and, no doubt, attractive. How does this match or not match with your understanding of Satan? How do you see evil working against God in the world and what is your response?
- The Garden of Eden is often described as a paradise. What would it be like to live there, had Eve and Adam not eaten the fruit? Would you welcome that possibility or not?
- Would it have been possible for Adam and Even to live fully adult lives within the confines of the garden? How or how not?
- Although Eve gets the blame for committing the first sin, what positive personality traits did she have, and how did they contribute to the foundations of the Christian faith?

To learn more about Eve, see page 164.

Sarah:

- Tenacious
- Possessive
- Spirited
- Resilient
- Weathered
- Proud

Text: *Genesis 12 - 23*

Setting: *The wild lands between the Persian Gulf and Mediterranean Sea, about 1900 BC - 1860 BC*

Significance: *"The mother of many nations," Sarah is the catalyst for the birth of Ishmael, borne by her servant Hagar, and bears Isaac in her ninetieth year, after she laughs at God when he predicts the boy's birth.*

Chapter 3

Sarah: No Laughing Matter

There are two kinds of old people in this world: those who stay home and die and those who don't even begin their life's work until their bodies hurt and start to wrinkle. I was plenty wrinkled by the time God got to me.

You see, something extraordinary happened to me when I was ninety. That's right, ninety — after twenty-five years of traveling through the wilderness, wandering, wondering, putting one foot in front of another, trying to keep the faith and trying to stay alive.

Where was I going? I wasn't always sure myself. You see, when my husband Abraham was seventy-five, God spoke to him. Not in a dream, not in a vision, just very clearly, passionately, in a do-it-right-now kind of voice.

"Abraham," said God, "you must leave your home. Go where I will show you. I will make you the father of a great nation, and by you all the families of the earth shall bless themselves."

Abe brought it up at dinner that night, casually, as if he was asking for another helping of lamb stew, his favorite.

"Honey, God wants us to pack up and leave everyone and everything. He's going to show us to a new land. And by the way, he says he 'will make me the father of a great nation.'"

I eyed him suspiciously. Clearly he was losing his mind. Maybe age was beginning to take its toll.

"The father," he said again, "of a great nation."

My eyes swept down to my sixty-five year old body, weathered and long past the days of making babies. Surely we were not capable of making one baby, let alone many.

We loved each other deeply, Abraham and I, but the one thing we wanted most in this world — a child — had never come to us. In those days having no children meant that your life counted no more than a grain of sand in the desert — one of millions, soon blown away, soon forgotten.

Abraham and Sarah were old, advanced in age; it had ceased to be with Sarah after the manner of women. Genesis 18:11

Of all the women I knew, I alone had remained childless, barren, empty. It goes beyond saying that it was my fault, for it was never the man's. Why had God punished me so?

I looked back at my beloved Abraham. He had never failed me, never given himself to another, never taken on another wife or slipped into a brothel in the various towns we had passed through. How did I know? I knew. Women know. Even though my skin was dry and my hair gray, Abraham convinced me that I was the most beautiful, most desirable, most promising woman alive. He really believed it. So did I.

I could see him looking at me now, calling me with his eyes. Did they still see as well as ever? No. The stars in the sky were dim to him at night; he complained of halos around them when there were none. He needed more rest than in years past and more time to get going in the morning. So did I.

Yes, some would say we were old, that it was crazy to set out toward the wilderness when we were only a short time from death ourselves. But this man I loved would never be old to me. If this is what Abraham wanted us to do in his seventy-fifth year, I would do it.

"God said we must leave right away," he said.

So we did. We said our goodbyes, packed our things, took our sheep and goats, servants, the relatives who were harebrained enough to join us, and left that very week.

✠

We wandered for years and years, through wilderness and desert, famine and strife. Maybe the course was clear to Abraham, but it wasn't to me. When he studied the nighttime sky for direction, I looked too — and wondered about God's promise of parenting a nation. Little by little, as nothing happened, I began to lose hope.

After ten years, it hit me like the surprising cold air of the desert at night: God had not made the promise to both of us.

"Abe, what did God say again?"

"That I would be the father of many nations. God said that I would have as many descendants as there were stars in the sky."

Over and over I reviewed those words in my mind. The more I repeated them, a glooming hole grew like a bottomless pit. One stark fact stood out: my name was nowhere to be found.

How could I have been so foolish, thinking I would mother a child at my age? How could I have even thought that Abraham and I would be the parents of a great nation?

There was one option. How I hated it. It had been rolling in the back of my mind for years like a burr under my clothes. By our laws, if one of our servants bore my husband's child, that son would be ours. Abraham would have a son. I would be a mother. More important, God's vision would be fulfilled.

I looked at the handful of servant girls who accompanied us into the desert. How does one think about sharing her husband? It shouldn't be that hard. Many men took more than one wife. And often when a man died, his brothers, in turn, took the wife into their homes, assuring her of children and a rightful place for those children, who would carry on their father's name. The system protected the woman and any children to follow.

I had never had to share Abraham. He had always been mine and mine alone. But God wanted us to have descendants too numerous to count.

I came up with a plan; I did what I had to do. I sent Abraham to the tent of one of my servant girls, Hagar.

Hagar was dutiful. Pleasant. I suppose I would have

considered her pretty, for her Egyptian heritage made her skin flawless. I didn't want to think about her skin. Or about my husband touching it. By our laws, if she had a son, that son would be ours. God's yearning would be answered; so would mine.

How I ached, time and time again, when Abraham entered her tent. I tried not to be aware of his comings and goings, but I knew every second when he was there and what he was doing. When he joined me, I felt like a crumpled rag, now discarded.

He tried to make it up to me, to take me in his arms and tell me I was his real love, that he was just with her so that we could have a child, that it was my idea. On and on. Logic.

It didn't help.

Don't get me wrong. Some of our men had two wives, even three. It shouldn't have hurt, but it did. More than I ever thought it could.

✠

Then the news came that she was pregnant with my husband's child. She would have a baby. His baby.

After all these years, the news should have made me happy, for I was finally going to be a mother.

I could not forget the fact that Abraham had joined himself to her. I reminded myself that it was my idea, after all. She's just a servant! It wasn't making love. It was just planting the seed.

I felt like a lonely dark planet orbiting solo. You couldn't see such planets, but stories had been handed down about them, how they were always alone, always murky and obscure, lost to the cold dark heavens.

For weeks upon weeks, months upon months, whenever I saw her, the look in her face was one of pure contempt. Full of arrogance, she had turned against me. Satisfaction seemed to ring the air around her, for she had lain with my husband and given him what I could not. One day I even backed her down with my hand.

"I gave her the privilege of sleeping with you!" I cried to Abraham. "Now that she is to bear your child, she despises me."

I heard myself say something totally illogical but that I could not help. It was if the words came from someone else's mouth. "God will make you pay!"

Where did that come from? Why would God make Abraham pay? Well, he should. Abe could have said no. If he really cared about me, he would have. *He must have wanted Hagar.*

My beloved took my face in his. "She is your servant," he said. "Do with her as you will."

The next morning I sent Hagar out into the desert. If she had showed one iota of compassion toward me, I would have let her stay. I would have welcomed her child as my own, but I could not bear her arrogance any longer. The younger women in camp were following Hagar's lead, and I could hear their taunts behind my back. Who knows? In my younger days, I might have made fun of an appendage too – especially a withered angry one.

Unfortunately, soon she returned and gave birth to a son, whom Abraham named Ishmael. Every time I looked at him, I burned inside.

The boy grew tall by Abraham's side, the heir to God's promise. I tried to be content, but there yearned within me a desire that would not be turned aside.

Then two strange things happened. Abraham came home one day and said that God was now calling him the father of not just one but many nations! This time I was finally in the equation. God had spoken of a covenant, telling Abraham, "I will give you a son by Sarah; she shall be the mother of nations; and kings of people will come from her."

God said to Abraham, "As for Sarah your wife...I will bless her, and moreover I will give you a son by her. I will bless her, and she shall give rise to nations; kings of people shall come from her."
Genesis 17:15-16

Kings of people will come from her.

Abraham told me that he had fallen on his face and laughed at God's words. With that, my heart fell, dipping below the horizon, leaving nothing but darkness behind. It was one thing to lose faith in myself. It was another for him, my beloved, to give up on me.

✠

Like the desert winds, the months and years blended into one another. There was no son born to me. Life went on the same, day after day after day. So it was almost with welcome relief one afternoon, some twenty-five years into our long desert trek, that three men approached us, seeming to turn up right out of the desert sand.

In those days, visitors meant one thing — you stopped what you were doing and gave them the best of what you had. Once they entered your tent, you protected them with your life.

Abraham ran, as fast as his old legs could carry him, and selected a fine young calf for dinner. While the servants grilled it, I lingered behind the tent wall where the men talked.

It wasn't really eavesdropping, because they were right on the other side — well, perhaps it was, a little. Maybe a lot.

I heard my name. Like a spider building a web unseen, I leaned closer.

"We will return in a year," one said, "and then Sarah will have a son."

What? A son? I looked down at myself, at my ninety-year old body with shame.

A baby! To have the pleasure of both making a baby and having one — that was something that had long passed me by. After all these years, God had never answered my prayers. Why should he now? Although Abraham and I still made love, my body was dried up like an old prune. Prunes don't have babies. Or maybe they have baby prunes.

The thought of me giving birth to a prune was so half-baked that I began to laugh and could not stop. The absurdity of all the years and all the promises hit me like a camel would, if it were to rise out of a piece of sand. I could hold still no longer. I laughed until my body shook.

The sudden silence on the other side echoed like a gong.

I had been found out — listening in and then laughing at what our guests had to say!

Sarah laughed to herself, saying, "After I have grown old, and my husband has grown old, shall I have pleasure?" Genesis 18:12

My actions were insulting, to say the least.

"Why did she laugh?" one demanded of Abraham.

"Why did you laugh?" he asked me.

I drew my body up to my fullest height — which was actually quite short — but it was all I had going for me at the moment.

"I did not laugh."

"We heard you."

"No, I didn't."

Ah, it was a bad day. First eavesdropping, then lying. Abraham was furious. I wasn't too happy myself. Before I could gather myself, they disappeared.

✠

In another year, the most wonderful thing happened, just like the men had said. I gave birth to a son, finally, my own true son. There I was, ninety years old and a new mother. We named the boy "Isaac," which means laughter.

And then we knew that our visitors weren't men, but angels. No wonder they had seemed to materialize right out of the sand.

Now Sarah said, "God has brought laughter for me; everyone who hears me will laugh with me...Who would have ever said to Abraham that Sarah would nurse children? Yet I have borne him a son in his old age." Genesis 21:6-7

Isaac's children and grandchildren grew up to be the Jewish people, of which there are as many as there are stars in the sky. And kings? I indeed was the mother of kings: David and Solomon and then the greatest king of all, Jesus.

With motherhood can come burdens: jealousy and possessiveness. One day when I saw Ishmael playing with Isaac — well, teasing Isaac, I thought — I exploded. No more. After waiting almost one hundred years for a son, I would not have this older one, Hagar's son — Abraham's firstborn — lord over mine and be the heir to God's promise!

Who knows? Had she been kinder towards me, things might have turned out differently. After talking with Abraham, I saw that he sent them both, Hagar and Ishmael, out into the desert. I assumed God would watch over them. All I knew is that I could not look at that woman and her son in my household any longer.

It is not always noble, this following God business. Sometimes you have to trust that God will use even our bad sides to achieve His ends. It tugs at my heart. I pray so....

Hagar

Sarah thought I was arrogant. She thought I was treating her with contempt. She thought I had risen above my fate.

Maybe I had. I had never been so happy. I was gliding instead of walking, beaming with new life inside of me, soaring above my normal tasks of cooking and cleaning.

For I was with child. Not any child. I was with child from the man who headed our tribe, our people. While some considered him remote, I saw one who breathed deeply the Spirit of God. Sometimes he was gone for days at a time, talking with God, listening to him. When he came back from those journeys, he reminded me of a well, a deep clean well full of vigor and health and purity.

When Sarah sent him into my tent, I knew how hard it was for her. There was never any question of him loving me. Or was there? She was his real love, his only love. I knew that. I was just grateful that he treated me kindly and respectfully, which was more than some men would have done. I like to think I brought him joy.

He didn't have to force me, although he could have. No one would have come to my rescue. By rights I belonged to Sarah; by rights a baby fathered by Abraham would become their child, not mine. By rights...well, I had few rights.

I remember his first visit, how we talked, an unexpected gift. How I took a deep breath — I had never been with a man before — and undressed. He was gentle. Then he was gone. Month after month came and went. He became familiar to me, intimately familiar. I began to look forward to his visits. Perhaps that showed in my eyes.

Then the day came that I realized I was pregnant. I ran to Sarah to report the news, expecting her to be overjoyed that she finally would have a child. I knew it would be a son; I knew that was what she wanted.

Cold silence. I could see her struggling with it. I almost wanted to throw my arms around her in celebration as the news that she would be a mother sunk in. I was only a girl, though, a servant girl; I kept my distance.

A fire banked flares up without much fuel. She was like that, for an anger started in her that day that never went out, igniting easily over the next few months as I grew larger and larger with my child. Well, their child.

I was so caught up with the life inside of me that I floated over my chores and responsibilities. Perhaps that was my undoing. When the baby started to move inside of me, I pretended he was dancing, as I was. I had always been alone, but now I had a partner in that dance, another person, another soul, right next to my heart.

Sarah grew angrier and angrier. I began to worry about my safety. Finally, after one particularly brutal day with Sarah's tongue and the back of her hand, I ran away. My people were from Egypt, and I thought, mistakenly, that I might jump on a caravan headed there. Once the temperature dropped that night, I knew I had made a mistake.

"Return home, Hagar," came a voice from heaven. "Submit to Sarah, at least for now." So I did.

When the baby was born, they named him Ishmael. As I held him to my breast, I knew I had never loved anyone as I loved him.

Over the next few years, I could see Sarah trying to love him, trying to reach out, to play with him, to teach him about his people and about God. There was no question that he preferred me, though, laughing and squealing, jumping into my arms.

Finally she chose to take it no longer. After Isaac was born, I knew she wished Ishmael had never been conceived, that she had never sent her husband to my tent. Abraham looked at me from time to time as if to say "I'm sorry," but left all the decisions up to her. Except when it came time to send me away.

Without warning, one morning he packed me off into the desert. He gave me food. He gave me water. Without my plan and God's protection, we would not have made it. I had made sure the boy knew how to survive by bow and arrow, and that's just what we did for quite some time in the wilderness. When he was old enough, I found him a wife among my old people, the Egyptians.

Ishmael grew to be a great man. From him — from me, the lowest of the low — and from Abraham, the father of many nations, came just that: another nation of people, the northern Arabic people.

...and the angel of God said... "What troubles you, Hagar? Fear not...arise, lift up the lad, and hold him fast with your hand; for I will make him a great nation."
Genesis 21:17-18

With him, I had made a difference. No longer was I just a servant girl that would vanish into the mists of time. I was a mother. Like Abraham and Sarah, I was a nation-starter.

After Sarah died, Abraham came to visit. Not me, but Ishmael. His eyes were filled with pride as he glanced at our son, but I also saw some sadness there. Perhaps he regretted sending me away. I'd like to think so.

I do not regret having Ishmael; on the contrary, he was my greatest joy. Age brings with it maturity. I have forgiven them for sending us into the desert; I have found that peace which passes all understanding. For I have seen what God has done, what God started back there in those desert sands. He has created generations of people that look to him in hope. I am at the front of the line, celebrating that hope — for I have seen what God can bring when all seems lost.

Sarah and I never found peace in this lifetime, but our sons will always be linked for they are brothers. I pray that their sons and daughters — and our millions of descendants — do find that peace. I pray without ceasing.

Why does Sarah matter today?

Sarah teaches us that we are never too old or too limited to make an impact in God's world. Rather than winding down as old age grew near, she struck out on an adventure that would put bones and flesh on God's vision of populating the world with sons and daughters of faith.

What learnings might Sarah inspire?

- Sarah had a magnificent sense of humor, which helped her break out in laughter upon hearing she would bear a son in her ninetieth year. Such a characteristic no doubt helped with the trials and challenges of nomadic life. Have there been times when laughter has helped you through a difficult situation? If not, how could such a trait be cultivated?
- Some have criticized Sarah for not being patient enough, not waiting upon God long enough. Do you agree or disagree? Why or why not?
- Why did Sarah feel the way she did after encouraging Abraham to sleep with Hagar? How did God act in Hagar's life?
- From Abraham and Sarah come the beginnings of both the Islamic and Judeo-Christian faiths. Can the knowledge of this story, through both its initial discord and eventual unity, help with understanding the current situation in the Middle East today? If so, how might learnings be applied?
- Sarah's story is full of emotion: laughter, love, jealousy, and anger. Has your reading of her story changed the way you look at her or any other biblical characters? If so, how?

To learn more about Sarah, see page 166.

Deborah:

- Prophetic
- Bold
- Resolute
- Decisive
- Gallant
- Unyielding

Text: *Judges 4-5*

Setting: *Twelfth century BC*

Significance: *An extraordinary leader, Deborah served as prophet and judge, rallied the northern tribes of Israel to war, accompanied 10,000 men to the battlefield, and returned home safely to tell the story.*

Chapter 4

Deborah: Warrior and Holy Woman

Most stories begin with the beginning. This one starts with the end. You see, there was a brutal assassination that finished off someone important. It involved a woman with a tent peg. I thought I should tell you first. She was my hero, by the way.

While death is not my preferred way of doing business, I guess you could say I was responsible for a lot of it that day. Sometimes there is no option.

The very future of Israel was at stake. Almost one hundred years before that brutal day, Moses had freed our people from slavery in Egypt. Forty years later, Joshua brought us into the Promised Land. When we overtook Jericho, we were strong and united, fierce and solid in our love for God and for each other.

In the years since, my people had sinned against each other and against God. The very first commandment that Moses had taught us as he came off Mt. Sinai was this: "I am the Lord your God, who rescued you from Egypt. Do not worship any other gods but me."

Well, that wasn't happening. Some had married those of other faiths and gone over to them. Some were worshipping foreign gods, including Baal and Ashtar, which was more than forbidden. It was treason against our Creator, the very one who had made us and set us free.

God was punishing us for that, letting us suffer under the hands of wicked rulers. Jabin of Hazor, the Canaanite king, was surely a brute. It didn't matter if you were a man, woman or child. Beatings, murder, slavery, torture and kidnapping were all tools used to control us. Initially our people were filled with rage, then sorrow.

Reports would come to us with their terrifying details as town after neighboring town was raided by his men. Young women, just starting to bloom, were carried off to bear other men's children, never to be seen again. Young men, full of hope and strong of muscle, were struck down as though they were weeds.

✠

Gatherings were out of the question. Travel was dangerous. Drawing water brought us some pleasure, for it was there by the well that the songs of our people would be sung quietly, over and over, teaching our young women the faith and giving them hope as they dipped deeply for both sustenance and strength.

In recent years, however, even the songs seemed to have a melancholy tinge. Soon, I feared, we would dissipate completely, all hopes and dreams ended, God's covenant with us discarded like rotten vegetables.

✠

The whole matter kept burning in my chest. And I was not without authority, for God had called me to be a Judge. Others named me "a mother for all Israel." Day after day I held court under a stately palm tree in the hill country of Ephraim. Disputes, large and small, came into my court.

My dear husband, Lappidoth, earned coins as a local merchant in the grove right below where I worked. Sometimes I think he worked nearby just to protect me. To make sure no angry soul who I'd decided a case against came after me.

Our children would run back and forth between my tree and their father's colorful tent, laughing. Sometimes my mood went up as I listened to them, but most often I brooded about their safety. I looked at my growing daughters and thought of their cousins, Miriam and Zipporah, who had run outside our town boundaries just two moons ago, wanting to stretch their legs and bring home firewood. They had never come home.

Day after day, my people seemed to grow more despondent, almost dull. They reminded me of wet clay, unable to take shape or move. That was what troubled me most. It seemed Israel was doing nothing to protect herself.

What kind of mother would not protect her offspring? What kind of mother would watch her children be exterminated without fighting back? Settling conflicts was easy. Now the biggest challenge of all was nothing less than preserving the future of my people.

✠

The breeze from the hills was fresh and clean that spring morning, but I knew danger loomed just over those gentle mounds. In my daily prayers for several weeks now I had been hearing a single, strong message from God: You must fight now, while your people have strength. Over and over it played in my head: You must fight now, while your people have strength.

One day soon, Sisera, the commander of Jabin's army, would burst forth and overwhelm us, as he had done in the surrounding towns. His nine hundred iron chariots and tens of thousands of soldiers would be no match for our men.

There was only one warrior strong enough to lead us into battle with any hope of success: Barak of Kadesh. Summoning him, I poured out the words in my heart: "Go, gather your men at Mount Tabor, taking ten thousand from the tribes of Naphtali and Zebulun. I, in turn, will draw out Sisera. He will meet you by the River Kishon and I will give him

Deborah sent and summoned Barak...and said to him, "The Lord, the God of Israel, commands you, 'Go, you men and Mount Tabor...and I will draw out Sisera, the general of Jabin's army...and I will give him into your hand.'" Judges 5:7-7

into your hand."

Strong stuff, I know, though it was all coming from God, not me. God had placed the directive in my heart. All I had to do was pass the word.

But then an unexpected obstacle.

"If you go with me, I'll go," Barak said. "If you refuse, I will not go."

I stared at the man, our mightiest general. He was the warrior, not me. Stories of our people at war flipped through my head as I searched for a precedent of women in battle. There was none. Thoughts of my dear husband Lappidoth raced through my head. I thought of my laughing girls. What would they do if I never came back? Their freedom was soon to be at stake, perhaps their very lives.

Barak said to her, "If you will go with me, I will go; but if you will not go with me, I will not go." Judges 5:8

I thought of myself on the battleground, the sole woman among thousands of enemy warriors. Death didn't frighten me. Unspeakable wartime atrocities did.

One step at a time. If Barak needed me, I would do what he asked. My girls might grow up without a mother, but at least they stood a better chance to stay alive if I fought the demons.

"I will surely go with you," I said.

Then more words spilled out.

"The road on which you are going will not lead to your glory, for the Lord will sell Sisera into the hand of a woman."

Because Barak was altering God's plan, he would not be solely rewarded with the victory. Don't ask me why I knew that. I just did. In times of crisis, God makes things clear.

✠

So we went forth, followed by ten thousand loyal and true men, some on horseback, some on donkeys, and the rest on foot, all willing to put their lives on the line for God and our nation. I dressed carefully, strapping on borrowed armor. Family swords, hidden for twenty years, were pulled out from holes dug in the earth under sleeping mats. Daggers emerged. Bayonets were quickly fashioned.

When Sisera discovered that our people were massing on Mount Tabor, his warriors seemed to come from all sides. As his soldiers and chariots raced toward us, the ground rumbled and the air grew dark. Images of impending bloodshed rushed through my mind. Ours was a long shot.

Then a strange sense of peace came over me. God was with us, and would not let us down. March on, my soul, with might. March on, my soul, with might.

"March on, my soul, with might!"
Judges 5:21b

✠

Our swords drawn, we waited until they were almost on us. Sharp blades, anchored on their wheels, flashed out at eye level to prevent us from overpowering the chariots. As their arrogant, harsh faces came into view, we turned and raced down the mountainside to the Valley of Kishon below. Triumphantly the soldiers charged after us, thinking we were fleeing.

Then, the unexpected. A torrential rain — which I knew at once was God's work — broke forth, blinding all in its path. What had once been the perfect terrain for chariots — dry and unyielding — instantly became mud, halting both men and wheels. The River Kishon flooded

"The stars fought from heaven,
from their courses they fought against Sisera.
The torrent Kishon swept them away,
the onrushing torrent, the torrent Kishon."
Judges 5:20-21

instantly, just as the Canaanites entered it in hot pursuit. As they floundered, we launched our counterattack.

No prisoners were taken; the only mercy shown was a quick death. But as the final count came in — some 10,000 dead — we were short the most important man: Sisera. He had turned tail and fled.

Word came hours later that he had entered the tent of a woman, Jael, the wife of Heber the Kenite, one of the iron-makers that had no doubt fashioned some of Sisera's chariots. He had asked for shelter. She gave him shelter all right, offering him milk to drink and a quiet place to rest. And then as he was sleeping, she took a tent peg and shattered his skull with a single blow.

✠

There is one image I cannot shake from that awful day: Sisera's mother. I was told that she waited by her window for him to come home, listening for the sound of his chariot wheels, straining to hear the shouts announcing victory, eager to share in the plunder.

"Why is his chariot so long in coming?" she asked. "Why do the hoof beats tarry?"

Then she nodded, agreeing with the answer offered by a maid.

"That's it: a girl or two for every man. Carts of loot for Sisera. And yes, perhaps a beautiful scarf for me!"

Even though she was rotten to the core like her son, she was still his mother. She wanted her boy at home; she wanted him to win; she wanted a souvenir — even knowing that a throat must be slashed to get it. But Sisera would never return, his heart forever stilled by an unlikely warrior: a woman with a tent peg.

Jael

The horror of what I had done silently screamed at me. There lay Sisera, the general of the Canaanite army, dead in my tent, a spike driven through his temple. By my own hand. Dead.

Why was it so quiet outdoors? Why weren't the rest of the Canannites rampaging into the house, pulling me limb from limb? I knew then they must have gone down in defeat.

Death served him right. I had no pity; I was more than happy to have done the deed myself. Disdainfully I kicked at the brute to make sure there lurked no life within.

From his hands slipped a skein of goat's milk, now empty, which I had given him only a few minutes ago. My choice was to serve him or die; I knew that. After a momentous battle, he asked for water; I gave him what I had.

Milk and then slumber. Fatigue had emptied all strength from the man.

If you could call him a man. The word brute would fit him better. Or monster.

I knew him. He had been to see my husband, Heber, twice — once to order dozens of chariot wheels and frames, and then once more, ordering him to work faster.

Maybe that's why Sisera sought out our home when he saw the rest of his army unexpectedly flooded by the rise in the Kishon River. He thought he knew someone who cared.

He was wrong. Dead wrong, as it turned out.

The monster did not know that my people had been Israelites. They had accompanied Moses through the wilderness, across the Red Sea and the Jordan River. My family, though, had long ago broken from the discipline that Moses sought. We married those of other faiths; false gods came into play; we strayed.

You could say we were were lost. Maybe we were. But I never lost my faith. And now I wanted revenge.

Years ago, Sisera had his army had level the town where I grew up.

My father was killed; my mother and sisters were raped, then left to die. I hid in the fields, where I had been working since early that morning. All I could hear were screams. Then nothing.

And now I saw him limp over the hill. Instant loathing spiked bile as I watched him make his way toward our tent. He must have been looking for Heber. Perhaps he wanted to toast the dead Hebrews.

A plan began to form.

"Come in, my lord," I heard myself say. "Turn in here. You can rest here."

Only Heber wasn't home. Just me. An unrelated man in my tent was an invitation to death. For me, not him. Bowing, I averted my eyes.

"Give me food, woman! Food and something to drink!" he yelled, looming, blocking the door.

"Yes, my lord, yes!"

"And be quick about it!"

How was I to explain this? That the enemy was in our tent, at my invitation?

Heber, where are you? I've got Sisera with me. Here. Just the two of us.

Maybe it was best I was on my own.

I grabbed some goat milk from a cool corner of the tent. Knees shaking, I brought the skein to him. With great effort, he unstrapped his heavy armor, letting it fall to the floor. His skin was mottled with bruises and contusions.

Slowly his eyes began to roll. Exhaustion had caught up.

"Be here when I wake up, woman," he sneered. "Be here. I have plans for you."

And then he passed out.

I could have run at that point. Perhaps I should have. The girl who hid under her father's house would hide no longer.

Turning, I looked for a weapon...a knife, a club...and then my hand fell to what was closest, a tent peg. A tent peg, yes, and the wooden mallet for pounding out grain. I would nail this dog to the ground where he lay. Feeling rage and grief for the loss of my family, I stood over his sleeping form, then knelt quickly to his side. There in its sheath was Sisera's own knife; brutal, heavy, and cold, still fresh from battle, stained with blood. Hebrew blood.

Placing the peg to his temple I raised the mallet...hesitated...my father's face swam before my eyes, my sister's voice in my ear. The mallet smashed down and it was done. Barely a move from his body...the eyes had sprung open, but there was nothing behind them. The brute was dead.

Jael the wife of Heber took a tent peg, and took a hammer in her hand, and went softly to him and drove the peg into his temple, till it went down into the ground, as he was lying fast from weariness.
Judges 4:21

They said I was a hero. Deborah and Barak gave me the credit for the final piece of the battle. But I was just a woman into whose hands an enemy had fallen. Deborah had sent him there. No, it was the Lord who had sent him — into my tent.

Why does Deborah matter today?

In a time when women act as military or political leaders, Deborah found a way to do both, inspiring thousands to serve God and country. When peace could not be brokered, however, she did not watch the war from the sidelines: she led, with Barak, 10,000 warriors into battle to free the Hebrew people from oppression and violence. Together, men and women working jointly, they broke the back of the Canaanite army, at least for a time. True leadership demands the best of all of God's people, as this story so aptly proves.

What learnings might Deborah inspire?

- What about this story surprises you? Angers you? Intrigues you? How do you reconcile the brutality in the story with your knowledge of God?
- To what extent, if at all, does this situation resemble modern warfare? Was Deborah justified in rallying Israel to go to war? Was Jael justified in killing Sisera?
- Deborah was referred to in Judges 5:24 as "the mother of all Israel." What characteristics led her to have that name?
- The biblical narrative of Deborah's activities varies slightly from the ancient poem, the Song of Deborah, that describes the same events (Judges 5). The poem is known as one of the oldest parts of the Bible. Which account holds more meaning for you and why?
- Readers of the Bible throughout the ages have found Jael's actions particularly unnerving. What is your reaction and why?

To learn more about Deborah, see page 168.

Hannah:

- Self-sacrificing
- Faithful
- Eager
- Nurturing
- Persistent
- Expectant

Text: *1 Samuel 1, 2*

Setting: *About 1100 BC in Shiloh*

Significance: *Unable to bear children, Hannah bargains with God for a son. If granted her heart's desire, she will dedicate him to God's service.*

Chapter 5

Hannah: Holding Close, Letting Go

Her words slashed me like a whip: gouging, cutting, crippling. It wasn't the first time; the wound had been gouged open time and time again.

"You won't need extra food, Hannah," Peniniah hissed, sitting next to me. "I'll give it to MY sons." She leaned in, whispering. "You are barren, Hannah. What you do here never matters because once you die, you're gone forever. Without children, you're NOTHING."

Then she left, calling her youngsters to her, leaving me to clean up. They joined her outside the tent, her daughter skipping, her two boys throwing a carved boomerang back and forth. That toy might as well have been me: solo, a plaything, always on display.

Peniniah was right on one count. I wouldn't need the food. My husband's other wife, she made me so sick to my stomach that I could barely stand it.

"Don't give her another thought," chided Elkanah, our husband, his beguiling brown eyes dearer to me than anything. "Am I not better to you than ten sons?"

"Hannah, why do you weep? And why do you not eat? And why is your heart sad? Am I not more to you than ten sons?"
1 Samuel 1:8

I thought of how much I loved him, how much I wanted to see those eyes in his son, MY son. How I wanted to hold that child to my breast, to see him grow into a tall man like his father. To know that upon my death, I would still make a difference through him.

But month after month, year after year, my stomach lay flat like the desert, dry and preoccupied with nothing but its own survival. It wasn't that I felt like a failure without children; I WAS a failure. A complete bust.

✠

I rose quickly, pushed through the tent flap and ran to the temple, oblivious to the food and plates I had left scattered behind.

"Lord Almighty," I begged. "Please hear me. I beg of you – give me a son. I have always served you in my life and stand before you now, begging for a child. Please hear me; grant me a son."

Although God had heard me pray many times, this may have been the time I prayed the hardest. I was not backing off.

Hannah was speaking in her heart; only her lips moved, and her voice was not heard; therefore Eli took her to be a drunken woman.
1 Samuel 1:13

Hot tears ran off my face like oil on a skillet, marking the ground below.

"God, if you answer my prayer, I promise I will return my son to you, that he will serve you all his life. Lord, give me a son!"

Suddenly a voice bellowed from behind me. "It is wrong to come here drunk!"

Arrgghhh! It was Eli, the priest. I thought I was alone. Apparently not. I had been so deep in prayer that he had mistaken my anguish for drunkenness, seeing only my lips and arms moving.

"Throw away your wine! It is sinful to approach the Lord this way!"

I whirled around, my eyes cast low.

Just maybe he could help.

"I have not been drinking, sir," I said, trying to compose myself. "I am a woman in terrible pain and have been pouring out my heart to the Lord! All these years I have been unable to conceive and cannot understand why I must suffer this terrible burden. What have I done wrong? Why, why, am I unable to bear a son?"

As Eli grew calmer, I started to shake. I could no longer bear this heavy load.

Finally he took pity on me.

"Go in peace," he said, "and may God grant the request you have made."

My heart lifted. Perhaps now, finally, God would hear me.

"I am a woman sorely troubled; I have drunk neither wine nor strong drink, but I have been pouring out my soul before the Lord."
1 Samuel 1:15

✠

It was that time of the month again. I could tell by the lines I drew in the ground, behind the bed that I shared with Elkanah most nights, at least when he wasn't with the Goddess of All Fertility.

I prepared myself for the inevitable.

Only nothing happened. One day, two days. Seven days went by.

Could it be? No.

Another fourteen days went by. The moon and I had been friends for years; we were on the same monthly cycle, growing fuller, then waning. This time we were out of sync. Stress. I knew it was stress.

Plus I was getting older. Women skipped periods as they aged. That must be it. Age. The inevitable downside. Happening even sooner than I thought.

Either I was totally used up, off into the years where there is no hope left, or...or, or?

Over the next few weeks my breasts began to change, to grow a little, to hurt.

My God. Could it be? After all this time? After all these prayers?

I could deny it no longer when I felt the first stirrings within me. I was going to be a mother! Come what may, my prayer had been answered. God had acted.

✠

We named our son Samuel, which means "name of God." He was everything I had hoped for and more. I always knew I would love a child; I just didn't expect to be in love with him. I kissed his head — full of soft light hair from the start — over and over, breathing in his sweet scent as I held him to my breast.

Other babies, Peniniah's in particular, seemed fussy at the breast: on again, off again, crying, not seeming to care. Not my Samuel. Seven or eight times a day I would hold him close as he drank his fill.

Our sweetest time was in the early evening, rocking in the sling chair Elkanah had made for us. Shadows would grow dim on the wall as I held him, my life so inexorably linked to his. I knew my time with him would not be long, like other mothers and sons. One day soon he would stop nursing. And then it would be time to turn him over to be raised in the temple. But I would give him every second I had. Every touch, every gesture, every moment I had to share would be his.

Then the day came, in his third year, when he began to grow restless at my breast. My vow haunted me like a terrible windstorm, sweeping away all in its path. I sobbed as I held him close that night, my lips brushing his sweet head. How could I give up this boy, this boy who had touched my soul as no other?

Samuel reached out his small fingers to my wet cheek. Then he simply handed me his little woolen blanket, the one he slept with at night and carried with him during the day. I held it to my face, tears streaming, wondering how I could find the strength to let him go.

Although she may argue it inside, a mother knows when it is time to let go. For me it was horrendously earlier than I would have liked, but I still knew it was time. The next time Elkanah went to Shiloh to worship, I went along, my precious boy in my arms for the last time.

Hand in hand, we stood before Eli, the priest who had mistaken my sorrow for drunkenness.

"I promised the boy to the Lord," I said. "I am keeping that promise. For as long as this boy lives, I am lending him back to the Lord."

God bless the old man. He went down on one knee, looked into Samuel's eyes and nodded. Then he left us alone.

Kneeling, I embraced my son, wondering how I would find the strength to force my legs to leave him.

"For this child I prayed; and the Lord has granted me my petition which I made to him. Therefore I have lent him to the Lord; as long as he lives, he is lent to the Lord."
1 Samuel 1:27

"You have my heart," I whispered. "I will always love you dearly, more than anything. But you are alive because of God. It is he whom we serve."

If he had cried, I don't know what I would have done. He was brave, as I tried to be. Somehow I found the strength to take his little hand, walk outside, and put it in Eli's.

As they walked away, my feelings tumbled out like rushing water: torrential, jumbled, chaotic. I took life a day at a time, struggling to make it through what seemed like an unending gorge of emptiness. Elkanah held me close each night, ignoring the Goddess in the next tent. Finally I began to look ahead.

✠

Perhaps all mothers believe their children will change the world. I knew mine would, and he did. My little Samuel grew to be a priest, prophet and judge. And he did something else: he found and anointed the first kings of Israel, Saul and David. Under his guidance, Israel grew from a scattered people into a true nation.

After many tears, I found a bit of peace, knowing that I had kept my word, knowing that my son was at work in the world, knowing his life, and mine, would make a difference.

God continued to be good to me. Elkanah and I went on to have five more children, three sons and two daughters. Each day, though, I would find time to work on a coat for Samuel. I wanted him warm in that cold temple.

His mother used to make for Samuel a little robe and take it to him each year, when she went up with her husband to offer the yearly sacrifice.
1 Samuel 1:19

Bless him, Lord, bless my boy, I would pray, over and over, as I wove the woolen garment. The tears never stopped completely; they are plaited into the fabric. I missed him terribly. Each year as we returned to Shiloh to worship, I would see our son, give him his new coat, celebrate every inch of growth, and thank God that he was alive and healthy.

When he was twelve, he told me that God had called to him as he slept — over and over. He did not know it was God at first, until Eli told him to listen clearly and say, "Speak, Lord, for your servant hears." When Eli heard what God had to say, the words chilled him to the core.

That is another story for another day.

Sometimes I do wonder what would have happened if I had kept him to myself. For some that would have been an option; for me, it was not.

I made a promise to God — the God who accompanied me from birth, walked with me through the valley of depression and fear, and gave me the greatest gift of all: my son.

I kept that promise.

Why does Hannah matter today?

Hannah petitioned God, publicly and privately, for her heart's desire: a son. Seeing her prayer answered, she never forgot her promise — to give that son in service to God — and left Samuel at the temple to be raised as would be best for him, and for God. Determined to put her love for God ahead of herself, Hannah exemplifies self-sacrifice and faith.

What learnings might Hannah inspire?

- What must it have been like for her to give up Samuel? Are there experiences in your life where you let something or someone go in God's hands? What was the outcome and to what extent did that change your relationship with God?
- Hannah poured out her heart to God in prayer, and her prayer was answered, just as she had hoped. Has that happened to you and how? Have there been times when you felt your prayers were not answered or answered in a different way from what you wanted? Did your sense of things change over time?
- Compare the Song of Hannah with the Song of Mary, noting how they are both uttered in thanksgiving and anticipation and how God is praised for liberating his people from oppression. What are some other themes that strike a chord with you?

To learn more about Hannah, see page 170.

Ruth:

- Hungry
- Hardworking
- Eloquent
- Loyal
- Vulnerable

Text: *The Book of Ruth*

Setting: *Moab and Bethlehem, about 1120 BC*

Significance: *In a stellar illustration of faith and self-sacrifice, Ruth, a young woman and new widow, accompanies her mother-in-law Naomi to Bethlehem, Naomi's home, leaving all that is familiar behind.*

Chapter 6

Ruth: Lighting the Way

It wasn't the days that were hard; it was the nights. The darkness lay on us like a frozen blanket, not cold enough to kill us but enough to rob us of sleep. Not that we were sleeping much anyway. Eyeing us like meat, other travelers seemed always ready to pounce, to steal us away. Unaccompanied women, on a wilderness trek or through life itself, were fair game for much worse than I can tell you here.

So what was I doing, along with my sister-in-law, Orpah – day after day, following a white-haired, bent-over, stubborn woman named Naomi? We were asking ourselves that by the minute. My own people lived in Moab, some forty miles from Bethlehem, Naomi's home and destination. I had married her son, Mahlon, in Moab, and thought that was it. Until now.

For ten years, my husband had protected me, sheltered me, brought food home and drew me into the circle of his kin: his mother and father, his brother Chilion and Orpah. Then without warning, the men of the family died, leaving us bereft. I cannot tell you why, for we knew not if it was plague or pestilence or heavenly wrath. All we knew was an abject emptiness: hollow hearts, bare cupboards, and a sudden vulnerability. Neither Orpah nor I had borne children. Our arms were as empty as our hearts.

✠

We watched the old one, slowly putting one foot in front of the other. Each step was a huge effort. Even if we reached Bethlehem, then what? I had an entire family behind me in Moab; Naomi had only distant relatives in Bethlehem. Begging or prostitution were often the only options for widows.

Suddenly she slowed then turned to face us, her small feet digging into the dirt. "My daughters," she said, "it is time for you to return to your mothers. You must start a new life, for you have no future with me. May God grant you peace and healing."

She came to each of us, holding our faces in her hands, kissing our cheeks.

"Turn back now," she said.

Yes, this woman was stubborn, but in that stubbornness was *hesed* – sacred kindness. I knew she wanted the best for us, and we for her.

"We are going with you," I said. "We won't leave you alone."

"Turn back," she ordered. "Go your own way. God has dealt with me harshly, but you still have full lives ahead of you. I CANNOT give you any more sons. Go back to your mothers. May God bless you with new husbands!"

I looked at Orpah. Like mine, her face was wet with tears. Then she glanced back toward Moab. The lure of home was just too strong. Trembling, she kissed us and walked away, her figure growing smaller by the minute. I could not blame her. The scenario ahead was unknown and bleak; home was at least familiar.

I turned to console Naomi, but she had already left. Her traveling bag under her arm, she strode ahead, her head high, her steps inching along yet resolute. She would reach the land of her ancestors or die trying.

And most likely she *would* die trying. As the crow flies, forty miles is not much, at least for the young. But first she had to descend some four thousand feet to the Arabah Valley, the lowest spot on earth. Thirteen miles of dust and heat from the valley floor loomed ahead, *then* the climb back up and out to the wilderness of Judea. Only after that would she reach Bethlehem.

In that moment, I realized I would not let her die. She truly had become my mother.

As I caught up to her, words that I didn't know I had within me poured forth.

"Entreat me not to leave you or to return from following you;
for where you go I will go,
and where you lodge I will lodge;
your people shall be my people,
and your God my God;
where you die I will die,
and there I will be buried."

Naomi only sighed and shook her head. I swear the wrinkles around her eyes became more relaxed, her stride a bit longer.

✠

We walked for almost a week, rationing the small bits of food we had brought with us: dried figs, hard goat cheese, olives, and bread. Travel is not easy for an old woman; it is humbling for a young one as well. Jeers from groups of men seemed to surround us on every side. At night I hid my knife under my clothes; I would not go down without a fight. By the time we reached the outskirts of Bethlehem, we were famished and bone-tired.

"Do not press me to leave you
or to turn back from following you!
Where you go, I will go;
Where you lodge, I will lodge;
your people shall be my people,
and your God my God.
Where you die, I will die —
there I will be buried.
May the LORD do thus and so to me,
and more as well,
if even death parts me from you!"
Ruth 1:16

Naomi was as depressed as I had ever seen her.

"Is that Naomi?" asked an old acquaintance. "Have you come home?"

"The Lord has made life bitter for me. I went away complete, but came home empty. Clearly he has made me suffer."

I held my tongue. When she had left Bethlehem ten years ago because of famine, she rode on a donkey beside her husband and two handsome sons. Her stomach may have been empty but her heart was full. Now the only vestige of her past was me.

It was up to me to find us food. In a hurry.

"When you reap the harvest of your land, do not reap to the very edges of your field or gather the gleanings of your harvest. Leave them for the poor and the alien. I am the Lord your God."
Leviticus 23:22

Thankfully, it was late spring and the new crops were ready for harvest. I had spotted a particularly lush barley field on the way into town, and hoped to follow the age-old tradition of the poor, gleaning from the field whatever grains the workers had left behind.

I arrived at the field as the sun rose the next day, and received permission from the overseer to work the edges. Trying to avoid the leers that continued to grate on my soul, I toiled quietly, head down, facing away from the men harvesting the field. It was a delicate balance; I must follow closely enough to fill my sack, but not irritate the other women who had been working the field for days.

I planned to take the grain back to Naomi, who waited with other homeless women in a corner of the city. There we would trade the barley for other food scraps, make it into bread, or add it to a common pot for gruel.

As the sun rose high, so did the heat. I had brought no water, for my only thought was to go after food. Every sheaf I spotted I picked up; every grain left behind went into my bag. But months of grief and weeks of hunger began to catch up, leaving me dizzy and tired.

In that moment of exhaustion, I thought of Mahlon. He would not want me to die here. Like most marriages, ours was based on practical reasons: we were a good match. Over the years, I had come to depend on him, trust him, and yes, love him. Mantra-like, I drew strength from him to bend, reach and walk, bend, reach and walk.

Soon, a small gathering of paid workers surrounded a well-dressed man who seemed to be pointing at me. I kept working.

Suddenly the man walked over and introduced himself as Boaz, the owner of the field. Unmarried men and women were not to talk directly to each other, so I averted my eyes.

"Listen, my daughter," he said, "do not go to another field to glean. Stay in this one and follow close behind the workers. I have ordered them not to bother you."

I swallowed hard. Why was this man taking such an interest in me? Why was he calling me "daughter"?

"One more thing. If you get thirsty, go to the water jugs and help yourself."

The toil of the last few weeks and the grief of recent months boiled within me.

"Why are you being so kind? I am nothing but a foreigner to you."

"I hear that you have been merciful to your mother-in-law," he said, "and how you left your mother and father and all that was familiar so that she would be protected. May the God of Israel watch over you!"

✠

My sack filled quickly that afternoon as the workers left spare grains, even entire sheaves of barley. Boaz must have said something. Because of his kindness, we would get by. For now.

The sack I lugged home that first day drew Naomi's quick attention. Like a cat with a mouse, she pounced.

"Where did you work today? Did someone help you?"

"The man whose field I gleaned was named Boaz."

Her eyes filled with light.

"Blessed be the Lord our God! He has not given up on us after all. That man is a relative of ours. Keep working his fields, my daughter."

So she knew this man. Something about the tone of her voice gave me pause, but I said nothing.

Day after day, the routine was the same, with the wheat harvest following the barley crops. Each morning I would rise early; each evening I returned with a full sack of grain. I knew Boaz was looking out for us in body as well as spirit, for he had ordered his men to stay away from me, to not harass me as many female workers were harassed on other fields.

✠

Slowly I began to know joy again. I think Naomi felt the same. As our faces grew less gaunt, her spirits lifted.

"I have a plan," she said. "It's time for you to begin thinking about a new life."

I winced. Only a few months had passed since Mahlon's death.

"Trust me," she said. "He will not live on if you do not move ahead."

I knew what she meant. Jewish tradition held that the name and spirit of the deceased would be carried on if a new marriage took place with a relative. When a man died, a brother would take his widow for a wife, sparing her a life of destitution and raising any sons for his brothers as legal heirs. Mahlon's brother was dead. That was lucky. I wouldn't have wanted to marry him anyway.

> *"When Boaz lies down, observe the place where he lies, then, go and uncover his feet and lie down; and he will tell you what to do."*
> Ruth 3:4

Although such a union was unlikely, Boaz was a different matter. I thought of how he had provided water, food and protection. I felt safe near him.

"Put on your best clothes," Naomi

said. "You must have something left that looks decent. Go up to the threshing floor tonight, for there you will find Boaz winnowing the new barley. Don't reveal yourself until he has finished eating and drinking. But see where he sleeps and then lie down next to him. And then he will tell you what to do."

Was this woman suggesting I throw myself at Boaz? That I seduce him? That I open myself to ridicule or harm?

The look in her eye said yes. I couldn't believe it. God knows why I did what she asked, slipping into a worn but clean dress, anointing myself with a bit of fragrance for which she had bargained.

✠

Any harvest is cause for celebration, and the mood on the threshing floor was no different. As the grain was winnowed from the chaff on the hillside over the village, music from the lyre and tambourine mingled with lusty song as the men worked side by side, finishing months of backbreaking work and celebrating with food and drink, toasting the season's harvest. I watched from the shadows, nervous that I might be spotted. Boaz finally laid a blanket behind a large pile of grain, filled with the fruits of the harvest. Once I heard snores from the other men asleep on the floor, I made a run for him, curling up at his feet as Naomi had suggested. Several hours later, he awoke, trembling, as he felt me near him.

At midnight Boaz was startled, and turned over, and behold, a woman lay at his feet! He said, "Who are you?" And she answered, "I am Ruth your maidservant..."
Ruth 3:8-9a

"Who are you?"

"I am Ruth, your servant. Come close to me, pull your cloak over me."

The man could have raped me, thrown me out on the floor for bait, or sent me home alone through the dark streets. Good man

So she lay at his feet until the morning but arose before one could recognize another; and he said, "Let it not be known that the woman came to the threshing floor."
Ruth 3:14

that he was, he wrapped his arms around me, holding me close. My eyes filled with tears, the first since I stood with Naomi on the road to Bethlehem months ago.

"You are a woman of worth," he whispered. "I am honored that you have chosen me over the young men. I will do all for you that you ask."

Before the sun rose, Boaz filled my sack with six measures of barley and sent me away while the others slept.

The same question I'd heard the night before was tossed at me first thing, this time from Naomi.

"Who are you?"

Are you Ruth, the single one, the one filled with sadness? Or are you Ruth, soon to have a future?

I told her what had happened.

"Boaz will do the right thing," she said. "Wait."

✠

Later that day he sought me out, having won an argument with the town elders. Facing down a younger relative who had first "rights" to me, Boaz negotiated the steps necessary to take me home. Hope was not just an empty shell this time, for soon after we wed, I gave birth to a beautiful baby boy.

When Naomi held him for the first time, a wonderful thing happened. Women of the town gathered around her, saying, "Naomi has a son! Naomi has a son!" They suggested a name: Obed.

They could see her joy and so could I. But she had more than joy. She had friends. She had family. Her future was secure, as was mine.

The image of the solitary figure on the road flashed in front of me: a stubborn woman who dug her feet in, who would not give up her goal of getting home, who was willing to risk all she had to get there. She would go to her grave knowing that she had chosen the right road — the road that led her home, in mind and body and spirit.

Journeys often take us far from the places we love, away from family and friends. In returning to Bethlehem, Naomi gave us a wonderful gift as Obed grew to father Jesse, who fathered King David, the bravest and most eloquent king Israel had ever known.

Some thousand years later, a great-granddaughter of ours many times over would also journey to Bethlehem, poor and homeless, under great duress. She too would bear a child: Jesus, the Son of God.

We all do our part. For me, it was putting one foot in front of the other and following the lead of a stubborn old woman. Thanks be to God she never gave up. Neither did I.

Naomi

> Naomi said, "Turn back, my daughters, why will you go with me?"
> Ruth 1:11a

I told them to go back. It wasn't because I didn't care. They were still young; they could still find new husbands and have children. They weren't spring doves, but they weren't old hags, either. Like me.

We were five miles outside Moab. They had been good to come this far. I had over thirty-five miles to go: wild roads, stretches of desert, rivers to ford, hills to climb.

The girls should be sleeping under warm covers, eating well, starting soon to look for new mates. They had been more than good to me. I had no complaints. Well, that was not entirely true. I was a member of the Mother-in-Law club, and we always have complaints. At least this one does! But even I knew that they owed me no more. They did not even owe me five miles.

Kissing each of them, I smoothed out Orpah's hair, always straggly, and took Ruth's cheeks in my hands for the last time. I told them I loved them, and I did. There was no question of that.

It was time for me to go. I was alone and I knew it. Death for me was no doubt the next step. I wanted to die at home, in the land that God had given my people, the land of milk and honey, the Promised Land. I would get there or die trying.

Head down, I continued northwest, toward Bethlehem. By myself.

So I thought. Small feet, petite like mine, caught up with me. From under my veil I could see them. Step. Step. Step.

I would not look at her face. I knew what it looked like, for it was burned into my mind. Burned into my heart. Dark brown eyes, smooth skin, straight dark hair with a tinge of henna-induced red. Small of stature, large of heart.

"Go back!"

"No, Mother."

"If you come with me, you'll be stuck with an old woman — a dead one, because I won't live that long! If I even get home, that is."

"Save your breath. I married your son. You're my mother now."

"Go back!"

"Give me that pack or I'll haul it off of you myself."

Hmmm. It wasn't just her feet that were like mine. They say that men marry women like their mothers and obviously my son had. Ruth was like that. Headstrong. Obstinate. And entirely delightful.

You might have thought I'd be pleased to have a companion. I wasn't. I really did love the girl and wanted her to grow old surrounded by family. Not alone like me.

"Save yourself, Ruth. There's a good chance you'll die getting to Bethlehem. We might get there or we might not."

"I know," she said. "I know."

God knows I wouldn't have made it without her. She saved my life. Literally.

"I don't need much to eat," she'd say. "I have a small stomach."

Her face grew thinner as the circles under her eyes increased. One night by firelight I saw her grab her abdomen in pain. It had to have been hunger.

When we finally reached Bethlehem, I thought old friends might have opened their doors to us, had us in, offered us food and drink, but no. They muttered, pretending to be out of earshot, their voices wafting through the air.

"Is that Naomi?" "What happened to her?" "She looks so old!" "She's clearly cheated death, but not for long!"

They turned their backs on me, as we had turned our back on Jerusalem ten years ago. Sure, there was famine, but we should have lasted; we should have had faith that God would provide. But if we had, I wouldn't have known Ruth.

We huddled together with other homeless women in a corner of the city. Day after day she went looking for work in the fields as a beggar. When she returned empty-handed night after night, my heart broke for her more than it did for me. I'd seen too much to be surprised.

One night, though, she came home with some red lentils, apricots and figs.

"Where did you get this?"

"Someone just gave it to me. God is looking out for us, Mother."

Really. People handed out such food to the poor as much as donkeys knelt down and crossed their little hoofs in homage to people like us.

Later that night I saw her finger her neck, suddenly bare, where for years had hung a simple necklace given to her by Mahlon. It was then that I realized she had sold it, traded it away for food.

I watched her sleep that night, covered with a threadbare blanket and realized that I had never loved her more. What did I do, an old woman with one dead husband and two dead sons, to gain a daughter like this?

God, Ruth is a good girl. Help us to make it; help us find a way to live, to make a home. We don't need much.

Miracle of miracles, I soon found out that she had begun gleaning in the field of Boaz, a distant relative. He was kind to her. Did he notice her beauty? Had he heard how Ruth had been so loyal to me? Or was he just a gentleman?

My mind went to work. Sometimes foxes succeed in clearing out the hen house; other times they are shot.

I thought, I planned, I prayed, I schemed. I trusted the basic goodness of Boaz, and I trusted God. He had brought us this far, but we're God's partners; we're not audience members, watching a play.

Still, when I suggested she lay down next to Boaz on the threshing room floor, I could barely believe what I was saying. What kind of suggestion was that?

"Wait until he has sated himself, Ruth. Then cuddle up next to him. Tell him to throw his cloak over you."

Forget about your reputation, Ruth. Maybe get raped. Maybe be the laughing stock of all Bethlehem. I could just hear them now.

The whore. She thought she could get Boaz to take her in. All he did was have at her and then throw her out. You know. To the other men on the floor. Then they had to stone her. What did she expect, seducing our men?

I could not stop my mind from spinning nightmares during the long hours she was gone. At one point I thought I heard screams coming from the hillside where the threshing floor had been built, but it was just the wind.

When she stumbled back into our little lean-to the next morning, weighed down by bulging bags of barley almost as big as she was, I could barely believe my eyes.

God provided for us, and not just for the two of us. God took the loyalty of Ruth and the goodness of Boaz and gave us a little child named Obed, who grew to be the grandfather of King David.

David had eloquent words in his soul and fierce fidelity in his heart. He never stopped protecting those he loved, whether it be his little sheep in the fields or the whole people of Israel. Where do you think he got those qualities from? Mostly from Ruth and Boaz, and maybe just a little from this fox, this sly old fox.

Why does Ruth matter today?

Ruth held tight to what she believed was right, accompanying her mother-in-law to a foreign land, where she knew no one and no doubt would be scorned because of her Moabite ancestry. Through her faithfulness, bravery – and yes, behavior that was a bit risqué – she secured both her own future and Naomi's. More important, she helped open Jesus' bloodline to yet another culture, yet a deeper mix of blood and different ethnic identities.

What learnings might Ruth inspire?

- Picture yourself, grief-filled, following a stubborn old woman to a strange land. What would be going through your mind? Have you ever committed yourself to a path where the outcome was so unclear? Where was God in that journey and what was the outcome?
- Ruth embodies total commitment in her care for Naomi. Are there people in your life for which you would risk and/or offer all? Has that brought you closer to God and if so, how?
- Like Rahab, Ruth was an "outsider" in Jesus' genealogy. Is that significant? What people in your family tree are out of the ordinary and how has that made a difference?

To learn more about Ruth, see page 172.

Shulammite:

- Passionate
- Evocative
- Sexual
- Focused
- Vibrant

Text: *The Song of Songs*

Setting: *Jerusalem and countryside, about 950 BC*

Significance: *Love, emotionally and physically expressed, finds its place in the Bible.*

Chapter 7

Shulammite: Love and Lust

Author's Note:
Many schools of thought exist regarding the authorship and composition of *The Song of Songs,* known as *The Song of Solomon* in some Bible translations. Some theologians say the author was King Solomon himself, describing his courtship and wedding banquet with a new wife, one of some 700. Others believe the poem is woven together from three to twenty-five fragments of poetry, collected from a number of ancient sources.

✠

This author believes that any reasonably sane woman would not be able to express, or even find true love as one of hundreds of wives. Thus, this premise seems likely: the poem's primary narrator is a woman in love with a shepherd from the hill country of Judea. The woman — still technically nameless to this day, as "Shulammite" most likely has to do with her geographical place of origin — has been brought to Solomon's palace in Jerusalem by the king's emissaries as a likely candidate for marriage to the king. Wishing nothing more than to be reunited with her poor but much-treasured love — a true king in her eyes — she tells her story of searching for him, loving him, and wanting desperately to be married to him, not Solomon.

The Song of Songs is unlike any other book in the Bible, for it is deeply and primarily romantic, evocative and sensual, suggestive and stirring. Given that the original prose cannot be told in a more compelling way, what follows are excerpts from this classic work; then, a story based on fact and fiction.

A tip: as in the course of real love, *The Song of Songs* takes many twists and turns; mere logic will not win the day here. So sit back with wine or pomegranate juice and some chocolate. Read slowly, letting your heart lead the way.

The Woman

Let him kiss me with the kisses of his mouth!
For your love is better than wine,
your anointing oils are fragrant,
your name is perfume poured out;
therefore the maidens love you.
Draw me after you, let us make haste.
The king has brought me into his chambers.
We will exult and rejoice in you;
we will extol your love more than wine;
rightly do they love you.
I am black and beautiful,
O daughters of Jerusalem,
like the tents of Kedar,
like the curtains of Solomon.

1:1-5

Tell me, you whom my soul loves,
where you pasture your flock,
where you make it lie down at noon;
for why should I be like one who is veiled
beside the flocks of your companions?

1:7

The Man

If you do not know,
O fairest among women,
follow the tracks of the flock,
and pasture your kids
beside the shepherds' tents.

I compare you, my love,
to a mare among Pharaoh's chariots.
Your cheeks are comely with ornaments,
your neck with strings of jewels.
We will make you ornaments of gold,
studded with silver.

1:8-11

The Woman
The voice of my beloved!
Look, he comes,
leaping upon the mountains,
bounding over the hills.
My beloved is like a gazelle
or a young stag.

2:8-9

The Man
Arise, my love, my fair one,
and come away;
for now the winter is past,
the rain is over and gone.
The flowers appear on the earth;
the time of singing has come,
and the voice of the turtledove
is heard in our land.
The fig tree puts forth its figs,
and the vines are in blossom;
they give forth fragrance.
Arise my love, my fair one,
and come away.

2:10b-12

The Woman
Upon my bed at night
I sought him whom my soul loves;
I sought him, but found him not;

I called him, but he gave no answer.
I will rise now and go about the city,
in the streets and in the squares;
I will seek him whom my soul loves.
I sought him but found him not.
The sentinels found me
as they went about in the city.
"Have you seen him whom my soul loves?"
Scarcely had I passed them
when I found him whom my soul loves.
I held him, and would not let him go until I brought him into
my mother's house
and into the chamber of her that
conceived me.

3:1-4

The Man
Your neck is like the tower of David,
built in courses;
on it hang a thousand bucklers,
all of them shields of warriors.
Your two breasts are like two fawns,
twins of a gazelle,
that feed among the lilies.
Until the day breathes
and the shadows flee,
I will hasten to the mountain of myrrh
and the hill of frankincense.

4:4-6

You have ravished my heart, my sister, my bride
you have ravished my heart
with a glance of your eyes,
with one jewel of your necklace.
How sweet is your love, my sister,
my bride!

How much better is your love than wine,
and the fragrance of your oils than any spice!
Your lips distill nectar, my bride;
honey and milk are under your tongue;
the scent of your garments is like the scent
of Lebanon.

4:9-11

The Woman
I slept, but my heart was awake.
Listen! my beloved is knocking.
"Open to me, my sister, my love,
my dove, my perfect one;
for my head is wet with dew,
my locks with the drops of night."
I had put off my garment;
how could I put it on again?
I had bathed my feet
how could I soil them?
My beloved thrust his hand into the opening,
and my inmost being yearned for him.
I arose to open to my beloved,
and my hands dripped with myrrh,
my fingers with liquid myrrh,
upon the handles of the bolt.
I opened to my beloved,
but my beloved had turned and was gone.
My soul failed me when he spoke.
I sought him, but did not find him;
I called him, but he gave no answer.

5:2-6

The Chorus
What is your beloved more than another beloved,
O fairest among women?
What is your beloved more than another beloved,

that you thus adjure us?

5:9

The Woman
My beloved is all radiant and ruddy,
distinguished among ten thousand.

5:10

His speech is most sweet,
and he is altogether desirable.
This is my beloved and this is my friend,
O daughters of Jerusalem.

5:16

The Chorus
Where has your beloved gone,
O fairest among women?
Which way has your beloved turned,
that we may seek him with you?

The Woman
My beloved has gone down to his garden,
to the beds of spices,
to pasture his flock in the gardens,
and to gather lilies.
I am my beloved's and my beloved is mine;
he pastures his flock among the lilies.

6:2-3

The Man
You are beautiful as Tirzah,
my love,
comely as Jerusalem,
terrible as an army with banners.
Turn away your eyes from me,
for they overwhelm me!

6:4-5a

Return, return, O Shulammite!

Return, return, that we may look upon you.
6:13

How graceful are your feet in sandals,
O queenly maiden!
Your rounded thighs are like jewels,
the work of a master hand.
Your navel is a rounded bowl
that never lacks mixed wine.
Your belly is a heap of wheat,
encircled with lilies.
Your two breasts are like two fawns,
twins of a gazelle.
7:1-3

How fair and pleasant you are,
O loved one, delectable maiden!
You are stately as a palm tree,
and your breasts are like its clusters.
I say I will climb the palm tree
and lay hold of its branches.
7:6-8

The Woman

I am my beloved's,
and his desire is for me.
Come, my beloved,
let us go forth into the fields,
and lodge in the villages;
let us go out early to the vineyards,
and see whether the vines have budded,
whether the grape blossoms have opened
and the pomegranates are in bloom.
There I will give you my love.
7:10-12

The Man
Under the apple tree I awakened you.
There your mother was in labor with you;
there she who bore you was in labor.

7:5b,c

The Woman
Set me as a seal upon your heart,
as a seal upon your arm;
for love is as strong as death,
passion fierce as the grave.
Its flashes are flashes of fire,
a raging flame.
Many waters cannot quench love,
neither can floods drown it.
If one offered for love
all the wealth of his house,
it would be utterly scorned.

8:6-7

The Man
O you who dwell in the gardens,
my companions are listening for your voice;
let me hear it.

8:13

The Woman
Make haste, my beloved,
and be like a gazelle
or a young stag
upon the mountain of spices!

8:14

Shulammite

I was held in the palace, King Solomon's palace. Trapped in his harem, a huge harem. The other women, at least as far as I could see, seemed to like being there. They reminded me of horses: lively, handsome, feisty horses. Buffing and cleaning and grooming themselves daily, they trotted about the grounds, snorting in the fresh air. Then they'd go back and comb their fetlocks. Palace life in Jerusalem seemed to be all they wanted. That and the chance to bear the king's children, to belong to something greater than themselves, to have their children go down in history — as one of what? Hundreds, thousands of descendants?

Or maybe they just wanted to sleep with the king. Every night they put themselves on display for him throughout the gathering rooms of the palace. Strutting through with great fanfare, he'd finally select one woman. She would rise, with shoulders back and head erect — the proud chosen one, at least for that one night. The others would go back to the royal stables and bed down for the night.

There was no doubt the king took care of his women — in Solomon's case, some seven hundred wives and three hundred concubines — providing them with food, shelter, protection and prestige. In return, they gave him, and the country, loyal and true descendants, children who were educated in our ways, children who had a genetic identity stamped on them from Day One. Maybe it was his way of achieving peace through conquest. It was no secret that he loved women of all cultures. Bumping elbow to elbow every day were Moabites, Edomites, Zidonians, Hittites, Ammonites, and, of course, Israelites. All were beautiful.

Did the women love him? Did they know the true meaning of marriage? Yes to the first; no to the second. In my mind, at least.

I was a bit of a rebel, I guess, although I never thought of myself that way. My goal was simple: to marry the one man I had always loved. To have him all to myself. To claim him as my own. To stamp my love for him

"Set me as a seal upon your heart,
as a seal upon your arm;
for love is as strong as death,
passion fierce as the grave.
Its flashes are flashes of fire,
a raging flame."
8:6-7

on my heart and on my sleeve and high on my forehead, for anyone and everyone to see. That person was not the king.

My heart's desire was a shepherd in Judea named Joab, a man whom I had loved since I was a young girl. We grew up together; we would escape from the others when we had the chance — hardly ever, as families were extremely protective of their daughters — and spend whatever minutes we could together, in the hills, away from prying eyes.

The only reason we had yet to marry was because my father hadn't given his permission. Women didn't have many rights in my day. I prayed every day that he would yield, that he would welcome Joab as his son-in-law. Running away was out of the question; I would bring scorn on my family forever that way. And I could be stoned should I step outside the family and marry on my own.

So I waited and prayed. Desperately I yearned for the day when Joab and I would be husband and wife. Only my dreams kept me going. I dreamed I was searching for him, up and down through the streets of Jerusalem. In my dreams the king's guards interrogated me, beat me, and brought me home from my wanderings. Still I remained true.

Some might think I was blind with love. I wasn't. The vision of my heart was clear and true like a meadow stream.

✠

The day the king's emissaries came to get me was one of the blackest of my life.

"Arise, my love, my fair one,
and come away;
for now the winter is past,
the rain is over and gone."
2:10a-11

My mother answered the door.

"Daughter, daughter!"

"What, mother?"

"The king wants you! His men are here!"

Her voice was suddenly one of delight, while bone-chilling dread filled my heart. The king wants me? No. It couldn't be. I knew girls who had been plucked and never seen again. They were probably still within the palace walls. Bearing children like goats.

"What about Joab?"

"Forget Joab! He's a shepherd. You have a chance to be Solomon's wife! You know he only goes for the most beautiful girls."

With that, I was packed off to Jerusalem to live with the harem. Thank goodness there was some time. For six months the women taught you the ways and wiles of palace life; for another six months you were bathed and scented and prepared. Prepared for him.

✠

Solomon himself found me one night and tried to woo me over the next few months. I don't know how he kept me separate from the others, but he seemed to. Food, flowers, wine, walks in the palace garden — all preparation for living amongst his huge and still-growing family.

Women of my time didn't have options about marriage. Solomon could have married me, kept me in the harem, raped me or had me killed. But underneath all the king-business of developing both the country and his extended family, he was a good man.

"You are altogether beautiful,
my love;
there is no flaw in you."
4:7

"You're a beautiful woman," he would say, brushing his hand on my cheek. "You're bright and kind and gracious. I want you. I promise I'll take good care of you."

The king was promising me a good life. The king wanted me to stay.

My answer was always the same: "Thank you, my lord, but I am not able to remain here. My life is elsewhere." I did not go into details; that's all I felt he needed to know.

Such a refusal was rare. My rejection, mild as it may have

been, made him more interested in me instead of less. He noticed me as I roamed the palace and its grounds; sometimes he would nod as I passed. I learned about the ways of a king, and surprisingly, about the ways of a moral man.

✠

One day I stumbled into his judging chambers, from which I had heard he ruled with justice and kindness. I hid behind a column to see how justice might be meted out, but was horrified to see guards holding a squalling baby feet first, swinging him like a pendulum.

Seems there were two mothers and only one baby.

"This is my son but she claims he's hers," wept a young girl, her red-rimmed eyes looking as though she had been crying for days. "Her son died, and she came and took mine when I was sleeping!"

The other woman, older, with lines running down her cheeks like gullies, screamed, "No, her baby died and she has stolen my son!"

"He's mine!

"No, he's mine!"

Solomon looked at them, each in turn, for what seemed like hours. Then, still dangling the child, his words chilled my heart.

"Guard, take your sword and split this baby in two. Give half to each woman. It's the only way to settle it."

Brandishing his sword, the guard motioned for soldiers to take the baby, legs splayed.

Standing tall, the older woman nodded, her approval apparent.

The guard raised his sword with both hands.

"No, my lord!" screamed the girl. "Spare the boy. Let her have him!"

Greedily the old one reached for the bawling baby. Solomon slammed down his gavel.

"Give this baby to the girl! She is his true mother; there is no other."

From that moment I understood what the others said: Solomon was a true king. A real king, one who used wisdom instead of force to rule his people.

I respected him. I almost liked him. But I did not love him. The women kept trying to get me over to their side, to Solomon's side. "You'll come to love him," one said. "He'll take such good care of you," said another. "Forget Shepherd Boy," said a third. "You'll never leave here."

You'd think they'd be jealous of each other, having so little to do with their days and even less with their nights.

Surprisingly, real jealously did not flare until the arrival of the Queen of Sheba from the east. Coming from southern Arabia, some 1200 miles away, she arrived in a caravan the size of a small town. Exotic and untried spices caught our senses. Camels by the dozen grunted and snorted, making their peculiar camel-only sound. Servants by the hundreds overfilled the palace's guest quarters. Solomon was delighted by one gift in particular: precious sandalwood with which to finish his pride and joy, the temple.

In the queen, the women of the harem met something they had not faced before: a woman who was an equal of the king — economically, intellectually, and spiritually. She needed him for one thing: safe travel for her merchants. Vital trade routes to Egypt, Phoenicia and Syria were controlled by King Solomon's empire. Without them, her country faced collapse. The queen set out to nail down that business relationship as if her life depended on it.

That may have been the reason she came. I know it wasn't the reason she stayed.

✠

She barraged Solomon with questions, said the servants who

listened in and then reported back to the rest of us. Some said she came to Israel a pagan, but left with an unexpected and richer gift than any jewel: knowledge and love of God.

"Tell me about this power you believe in, this divine power," she would say. "How could one force, one being, have created the world? How was it done, Solomon? What about the fishes of the waters and the reptiles of the desert? Did he make them? How? What about your people? What makes them so loyal? What keeps them together? Is it God or is it you?"

Patiently he would answer her questions, one by one. He was doing more than answering questions: he was turning her into a believer.

Perhaps it was the energy she took or the physical intensity she demanded, but during her stay, Solomon did not tap a single woman from the harem. He had met his match. Both king and queen were driven to serve their country, to keep peace and to unite. Which they did.

Stilled, the usual drumbeat of the palace was set on hiatus. Week after week, month after month, Solomon and the queen tarried and parried, intellectually and physically: over meals, on the palace grounds, in the king's quarters, on long walks about Jerusalem. Solomon had never seemed so satisfied, so energized.

✠

I arose to open to my beloved,
and my hands dripped with myrrh,
my fingers with liquid myrrh.
5:5

The morning of her departure came none too soon for the other women of the palace. We stood outside in the blazing sun watching the myriad of items being loaded.

Solomon was left a richer man, for the queen had brought with her some 120 talents of gold, along with other gifts. The wealth with which Solomon loaded her down was equally impressive: fine linens, precious gold chalices and tableware and rare jewels enough, it seemed, to line every road in Arabia.

And then I witnessed an event which all did not see. Because I was young and rebellious, the old women in the harem had pushed me to the front to keep an eye on me. What did they think I would do? Jump in the caravan if they weren't looking? It was going the wrong way as far as I could see, opposite from the hills of Judea.

"Dear, dear friend," Solomon whispered as he kissed her goodbye, "this is for you and for our son."

What? A son? She was pregnant?

I watched as he gave her a ring, a large black luminous stone, and placed it on her finger. She traced the face of it with her finger, kissed him, and glanced longingly toward the chambers they had shared.

"A lion," she murmured. "The lion of Judah."

We never saw her again, although I heard later that she indeed did have a son and named him Menelik the First. When the boy put the ring on his finger, so the story goes, he felt an overwhelming surge of energy go through him — one that knocked him to the ground — confirming his identity as the son of two powerful monarchs.

✠

The women could not be happier that the queen was gone, and Solomon soon returned to his former ways with them. There was a new saying around the palace, though, that they now used if they were particularly upset or irritated: "Who do you think you are, the Queen of Sheba?" They would then laugh, and took each day in stride, welcoming the idea of growing old within the palace walls.

Not so with me. My dream of marrying Joab grew stronger every day. Day after day, I yearned for him, drawing pictures in my mind of him on the lonely hillsides at home, protecting and caring for his sheep — the sheep that would one day produce enough income to support our family. Night after night, I dreamed of him, of those times we had been together, and the years ahead for which I so longed. With him. With our children. In our own small house that would be my palace.

Solomon stopped by my lounge chair one night while making his rounds.

"Your trial period is ending," he said. "Any change in your thinking?"

"No," I said. "My resolve is the same."

He suddenly grew quiet.

"He is lucky to have you," he said, with a faraway look in his eyes.

How did he know there was someone else? I realized then that he missed the queen. Love had changed him.

✠

At the end of six months, Solomon let me go. I arrived at home to find that my mother had passed away unexpectedly only two days before. Awash in grief, my father looked me straight in the eyes.

"Do you still love Joab, my daughter?"

I nodded as though my neck would break.

"Then I will not keep you from him any longer. I myself never knew what I had until it was too late."

Thanks be to God. I would miss my mother deeply, but my resolve for Joab was stronger than it had ever been.

Like Solomon, I had learned something during my time in Jerusalem. I learned that love is a sacred gift from God, fed and nurtured by the flames of the heart. It does not need money or rubies or gold to flourish. What it needs is this: two hearts that beat as one.

Why does the woman in *The Song of Songs* matter today?

More than any other figure in the Bible, the woman in the *Song of Songs* lifts human sexuality to new heights. There is no embarrassment or chagrin about what she feels for the man she loves; she expresses God-given yearnings and desires. Fidelity, true love and marriage underscore her commitment.

What learnings might she inspire?

- The *Song of Songs* is filled with sensuality and lust. What does its inclusion in the Bible say about those things? What does it not say?
- She is committed to the love of her life, the shepherd from Judea, and does not intend to share her life with anyone else, although her quest puts her at some risk. Have there been similar people in your life for whom you would risk all? Where has God been in that process? How did you know the right course to take?
- What is your sense of the relationship between this woman and her beloved? What clues lead you to that understanding?

To learn more about Shulammite, see page 174.

Rahab

Eve

Sarah

Deborah

Hannah

Ruth

Shulammite

Mary, Mother of Jesus

Well Woman

Martha of Bethany

Mary of Bethany

Mary Magdalene

Mary:

- Young
- Scared
- Protective
- Tender
- Trusting

Text: *Luke 1 - 2, John 19*

Setting: *Bethlehem, 1st century*

Significance: *Mary gives birth to Jesus under much duress.*

Chapter 8

Mary: A Long and Holy Night

The donkey
was tired and wet like me
for my water had broken
over him
though he was not in pain
I was

I wanted my mother
not this strange town
for there were no beds
anywhere

Joseph returned for the twelfth time
shaking his head, angry
there is no room
he said for the twelfth time

but I'm going to have a baby
as if he didn't know
it hurts
I'm scared
doesn't anyone see us?
how can there be no room?

I knew the answer
no one cared

I'll try again, he said

disappearing into darkness
people had streamed by us
for days
pushing around
getting there faster
it was all wrong
and had been since the beginning
I thought of the angel

> will you have God's son?
> what do you mean, God's son?
> God's son
> Jesus
> will you?

I am a virgin
it is not possible

> God's son
> Jesus
> will you?

the angel's face was different
bright, kind, earnest
in that minute
I trusted him
my heart said yes
I will
I will do it

then the pulsating force
the energy
the beating of a thousand wings
joy overhead

but now he was gone
and Joseph was too
maybe they had forgotten me

Joseph was a good man
most would have thrown me away
some would have stoned me
yet he did not leave
you are mine, Mary

I am yours
we will stay together
he is at my side again
leading the donkey
leading me

come
I have a place
underneath all this

a cave?
dark
the smell of animals
moonlight filling the space
one star starting to throb
like me

tears come again
pain tears me apart
but then it is gone
mostly

my boy fills my arms
he is beautiful

a star on fire
he needs me
and I him

I have him
and Joseph
light
warmth
we are safe
and that is enough

Mary

The angel. I didn't understand the angel, at least at first. He said his name was Gabriel, but who was paying attention to names at that point? I was fourteen. How does a girl-woman of fourteen wrap her mind and her soul around the idea that she is to bear the Son of God?

I think back to the day I first heard the news. That memory often keeps me going now as I enter my eighth decade. I am not alone, for John, Jesus' favorite disciple, has made me his mother.

Still, I am not whole.

My heart has a hole in it that has remained empty for almost twenty-five years. I desperately miss Jesus, my first-born. I want to reach out and take his warm cheeks in my cool hands. I want to see his long and beautiful fingers. I want to hear his voice and never have him leave me again.

✠

That day, so long ago, changed everything I knew. My family, like a number of others in Galilee, lived in a two-story house. You stepped down to get into the house; half of the first floor was below street level. That's where we stayed cool.

That's where I was that morning. Sweeping the dirt floor, back and forth, like normal people do.

Normal people do not see angels. Large angels. Room-filling angels. Mentally distressed people see large angels, but I've always been pretty much intact.

Gabriel did fill the room. Thinking back, it makes me laugh. His large, shimmering, white-energy body had to kind of stoop at first. You would have thought that God might have ordered a smaller angel, one that would fit the room, but that wasn't the case.

"Greetings, Mary!"

The voice was behind me. I didn't bother turning around. "Greetings, Mary!"

No. No greetings. My brother, The Irritant, is playing a trick on me.

"Greetings, Mary!"

His voice sounds really low.

Finally I turned around, broom upraised, to shoo my brother out; advancing, eyes half shut, holding the broom like a sword, dodging, waving, forcing The Irritant outside.

But it wasn't him.It was indisputably, undeniably, an angel. His energy was unmistakable. I'd never seen an angel, hadn't heard of one in Galilee, but there he was. A clear, beautiful, pure sound of music filled the air around him. I looked for my brother, for my mother, father, anyone, but I was alone. An eight-foot-tall angel and me.

"Greetings, favored one! The Lord is with you."
Luke 1:28

"Favored one, the Lord is with you!"

Whaaaattttt?

"The Lord is with you."

I turned and ran to the back corner of the room, all of about twelve feet away, my broom clattering to the floor.

"Do not be afraid, Mary."

I was afraid.

How could I not be? I knew about angels from the stories

handed down from my people. Images flashed through my head, my mind searching.

✠

There were angels of death. Like the one who went through King Sennacherib's camp, causing 185,000 Assyrian soldiers to die before they could destroy Israel. Or like the one who stood ready to purge Jerusalem in David's time, until God made him stand down.

There were angels that inspired men onto battle, like the one who did tricks and made fire spring up to get Gideon to go to war in God's name. There were angels who appeared only to animals. Balaam's donkey saw one and refused to move, causing the man to beat it but to ultimately listen to God. There were messenger angels, one that spoke with Elijah and another that spoke with King David. I guess they all bore messages, messages from God, whether they be captains of the Lord's army or animal angels or courier angels.

To the best of my knowledge, though, no angel had ever appeared to a girl. One had come to Sarah, but she was about 500 years old at the time.

The one in my house didn't look like an angel of death. He was trying hard to be kind, I could tell. He seemed smaller, although his wings still brushed the ceiling. The strange but compelling music reached out to me like a hand would, a gesture of peace.

Reminding myself to breathe, I stiffened my ninety-pound frame as tall as I could. I would not be intimidated in my own house, but slim were the odds that my life would ever be the same. I could tell that already.

"Speak, angel."

"You have found favor with the Lord."

Favor with the Lord.

At that moment, I didn't want favor with the Lord.

"You will conceive in your womb and bear a son, and you shall call his name Jesus. He will reign over the house of Jacob forever, and of his kingdom there will be no end."

I knew one thing. Conceiving in my womb was just not possible without a man. I knew that. Virgin. No husband. No baby. No chance. The angel was wrong. He could go away now.

"You will conceive in your womb and bear a son, and you will name him Jesus."
Luke 1:31

"How can this be, since I have no husband?"

"The Holy Spirit will come upon you, and the power of the Most High will overshadow you."

I would have a baby? God's son?

There was no precedent in my brain for this. Was there a precedent anywhere? Chaos washed over me like a river swallows all in its path.

No. I would have Joseph's children. My beloved Joseph's children. We were to be married within the year. I was spoken for.

"Do not worry, Mary. Do not be afraid."

✠

"Your cousin, Elizabeth, is also with child. She is six months along now. With God, nothing is impossible."

Elizabeth? My cousin? The one who seems about 800 years old?

Could it be true? How overjoyed she and Zechariah would be. They had wanted children forever, it seemed, but had given up long ago, about the time her teeth started to fall out.

For nothing will be impossible with God.
Luke 1:37

"Do not worry, Mary. Do not be afraid."

Again the words came to me. For that one holy and divine moment, all was right and good, holy and trustworthy. This was no divine writ, no takeover of my body. It would be my decision. Gabriel waited.

"I am the Lord's servant," I said. "Let it be to me according to your word."

"Here am I, the servant of the Lord; let it be with me according to your word."
Luke 1:38

And with that, the music around Gabriel turned into the sound of hundreds of voices. Somehow I knew it was a chorus. Somehow I knew that I had done the right thing. That I was doing the right thing. Honest to God, there was joy in that room — from top to bottom and all around; there was rejoicing. Heavenly rejoicing, you could say. A whole communion of angels rejoicing. Honest to God.

✠

It is from that place of honesty that I speak with you now. I told you I was old. That much is true, but there is more. I am near death, crippled and bedridden, lying with my face to the wall in John's house. My own children visit, but as Jesus so wanted, John took me to his home. He and his wife have taken good care of me.

The angel said to them, "Be not afraid; for behold, I bring you good news of a great joy which will come to all the people; for to you is born this day in the city of David a Savior, who is Christ the Lord."
Luke 2:10-11

Early each evening John comes to me, telling me stories of what it was like to be on the road with Jesus, how my son would cure the sick and lame, how he invited the little ones onto his lap, how he despaired when people would not hear about his father in heaven. He tells me about Jesus' friends: Bartholomew and Nathaniel, Peter and Andrew, Mary of Magdala, Mary of Bethany and her sister, Martha.

He tells me tales of Jesus laughing, loving, being whole. If I close my eyes and just listen to his voice, it almost blocks the image of my son collapsed on that cross, then dead on the ground. As hard as I try, I cannot shake that day for long. No mother could.

Being a mother — Jesus' mother — is who and what I am most of all. I don't know why God chose me; perhaps I never will. I do know this, though: I want to see my son again. I want to look into his eyes and put my arms around him and talk to him without millions of people around. I don't want him to leave me again. Ever.

✠

It must be getting late, for I hear John's voice. I cannot quite make out what he is saying, for he sounds far away, sad, distant.

There is something else overriding his words: music. Lovely, light, vibrant, elegant music. I haven't heard music like this since...since...

"Mary."

That voice. I know that voice.

This time I answer right away.

"Yes, Gabriel?"

The angel fills the room again, casting light that bounces off the wall in front of me as he touches my shoulder.

"Favored one, the Lord is with you!"

I can barely turn my head because it hurts so much, but I do. And he is not alone. There is someone with him.

My son.

Jesus has come for me.

At once I am up and going, reaching for him with arms that are no longer brittle but sturdy, almost as strong as they were as when I held him on that indescribably long ride from Bethlehem to Egypt. He catches me, enfolds me, and I am exactly where I want to be — with him.

John and his wife are in tears, but all they see is my thin, worn, used up shell of a body, now devoid of breath. Can't they see Jesus?

Can't they hear the melody? Can't they see how happy I am?

We step out toward the music, now increasing in beat and pulse, calling us, welcoming us. I have longed to hear that sound ever since I was a girl, so scared, so terrified.

Again I hear Gabriel's words: "Do not worry, Mary. Do not be afraid." I take his words to heart, for I walk with my son.

Why does Mary matter today?

God steps outside traditional boundaries throughout the Bible, and has done so here by asking a young, unmarried girl-woman to bear his Son. Through Gabriel, God sought Mary's cooperation; he would not have acted without it. Mary overcame her fears to participate in the greatest miracle of all time: Jesus' birth among us. Women are held up both at the beginning of Jesus' life and at the end of his mortal life; such affirmation comes from none other than the heart of God. Such an honor needs not to be taken lightly.

What learnings might Mary inspire?

- Mary had an extraordinary conversation with the angel Gabriel regarding the potential birth of Jesus. The choice of whether to sign on to God's plan was clearly in her hands. What would have happened if she had said no? Would Jesus have been born? Would God have sought another? Real free will indicates that God would not peek into the future, and that Mary's choice of giving birth to Jesus was truly that: a choice.
- Consider the meaning of free will in Mary's decision and the actions of Eve, who was the first to exercise it. Clearly there are differences; are there similarities?
- Mary has been venerated by many through the ages. What are your thoughts about her and to what extent does she make a difference in your life?

To learn more about Mary, see page 177.

The Magnificat

"My soul magnifies the LORD,
and my spirit rejoices in God my Savior,
for he has regarded the low estate on his handmaiden.
For behold, henceforth all generations will call me blessed;
for he who is mighty has done great things for me,
and holy is his name.
And his mercy is on those who fear him
from generation to generation.
He has shown strength with his arm,
he has scattered the proud in the imagination of their hearts,
he has put down the mighty from their thrones,
and exalted those of low degree;
he has filled the hungry with good things,
and the rich he has sent empty away.
He has helped his servant Israel,
in remembrance of his mercy,
as he spoke to our fathers,
to Abraham and to his posterity forever."
Luke 1:46-56

Well Woman:

- Smart
- Careworn
- Flippant
- Irrepressible
- Philosophical
- Tenacious

Text: *John 4*

Setting: *Samaria, first century*

Significance: *Bantering with Jesus, this unnamed woman is rewarded with a life-changing encounter in which he reveals he is the Messiah.*

Chapter 9

Well Woman: Drinking Deep

I could feel their scorn: women, inside their shadowy houses, pointing their fingers at me as I walked through town.

"Don't wind up like her," they would say to their daughters. "Five husbands! Ha!"

I stiffened my spine, as if heading into a yowling desert wind. The only time it really hurt was when they'd hold their girls back from me on the street, as if I'd contaminate them.

Although they were never rude outright, they did everything they could not to talk to me. When I appeared, their voices hushed. When I left, I felt their pointed fingers, their ridicule cutting into me like a dull knife, over and over.

I was hot and tired and irritable, for it was high noon. Most women went to the well first thing in the morning or right before sunset. I went at noon and used the old well outside of town so I wouldn't have to hear them.

I was as untouchable as a leper.

Well, excuse me. So my life hadn't gone exactly as planned as had theirs: virginity, marriage, children.

What about me was so terrible? Why had I been married so many times? What do you think it was like to lay with five different men, none of them caring about me? But only about what I could provide?

Let's try some scenarios.

I was crazy and five men threw me out.

I was infertile and no one wanted me.

Five brothers had me, one after another, desperately trying to have children, but died young.

I burned the bread. Really. Men got rid of wives for lesser

things. They didn't even need a reason. All they had to do was point toward the door and you were out. For good.

✠

Do the details of my life matter that much? They didn't to the man I met by the well. I'm not sure I care what you think, but that man — how I cared for him.

There he was — it seems like yesterday — sitting by the well with his head down. He was Jewish and he was bone tired. Two clues: the tassels on the bottom of his prayer shawl and his reddened and exhausted face.

As I lowered my jug into the cool water, I felt his eyes bore into the back of my head. No matter. I ignored him. Like I said, I was used to it.

Then the words: "Please give me a drink."

Please give me a drink.

Like a vase thrown from a rooftop, his words shattered the stillness. Was he talking to me? He had to be. I was the only one there.

You have to understand. Men just don't talk to women. Jews sure as hell don't talk to women like me, women of Samaria. They hate us. It's mutual, by the way. What's with that "please" thing, by the way?

✠

I'll never know why, but I decided to have a little fun with him.

"Sir, you have no bucket, and the well is deep. Where do you get that living water?"
John 4:11

"Why is it that you, a Jew, ask a drink from me, a woman of Samaria?"

"If you only knew the gift God has for you and who I am, you would ask me for that, and I would give you living water."

Oh, shut up.

"Sir, you don't have a bucket and the well is deep. Where do you get that living water? Like you're more important than Jacob, who gave us this well."

Silence. I knew I had him. Jacob was a patriarch, right up there with Moses and the others. We knew that he had used this well, and was buried nearby.

"Everyone who drinks from this well will be thirsty again. But if they drink the water that I have, never again will they thirst. It will give them eternal life."

"Sir, give me this water, that I may not thirst, nor come here to draw."
John 4:15

What? Who was this man? What was he talking about? Why was he talking to me? Men didn't even talk to their wives in public, let alone strange women.

I played along. This was kind of fun.

"All right. Fine. Give me some of that water — that eternal water — so that I never have to come here again."

Silence. He looked at me. I looked back. "Good" women weren't supposed to look at men. In the eye, that is. Maybe at their feet. Well, I was tired of looking at men's feet, and I was so far from good that it didn't matter anymore.

"Go, call your husband, and come back."

Jesus said to her, "You are right in saying, 'I have no husband'; for you have had five husbands, and the one you have now is not your husband."
John 4:17

Oops.

"I have no husband."

Then the zinger: "You are right in saying, 'I have no husband,' for you have had five husbands and the one you are with now is not your husband."

Whaaaaattttt? HOW DID HE KNOW?

My mouth hung open like a fish net. For once I had nothing to say.

"Sir," I finally squeaked. "I, um, think you may be a prophet."

A prophet? A prophet? Is that the best I could come up with?

Still my mind careened, trying to catch up.

"Our ancestors worshiped on this mountain," I said, pointing to beautiful Mount Gerazim, "but you say the place where people must worship is in Jerusalem."

Ha. Nice recovery, I thought. If this man is such a prophet, let him answer that! Only a REAL prophet would know that. Jews and Samaritans had argued for hundreds of years just where to worship God. They said Jerusalem; we Samaritans said Mt. Gerazim. They were wrong.

He looked at me again, that look-through-you thing.

"The time is coming," he said, "when it doesn't matter where you worship. Actually, the time is here. When those who truly believe will worship in spirit and in truth, it won't matter where your feet are."

"I know the Messiah is coming," I said quickly. "The one who is called the Christ. When he comes, he will explain everything to us."

✠

The woman left with her water jar, and went away into the city, and said to the people, "Come, see a man who told me all that I ever did. Can this be the Christ?"
John 4: 28

With that, I picked up my water jug, turned my back, and started home. An interesting conversation...but then the stopper.

"I am he," he said. "I am the Messiah."

I stopped cold. It couldn't be! And yet it all made sense. His ability to know the truth, his words about worship, the way he seemed to care about me...I had not been expecting that.

I knew that others had to hear. I was the one to spread the word, no matter what they thought about me. I had been given this gift. Flinging down my jug, I ran toward town as fast as I could...my hands free, my heart free, for the first time in a long while. I had much to tell about the man at the well.

Why does the woman at the well matter today?

Feisty and curious, shunned by many and yet not afraid, the conversation with the woman at the well demonstrates a central truth: Jesus valued women and their intellectual and theological contributions. This story also demonstrates that Jesus appreciated, and had, a good sense of humor.

What learnings might the woman at the well inspire?

- Why did Jesus take so much time with this woman? What about her appealed to him?
- Freedom of speech was no stranger to her, at least in this conversation. What might have motivated her to respond and parry as she did? What does that indicate about your relationship with God, if anything?
- What traits do you admire in her? Do they resemble any in yourself? How might you use those traits in God's service?
- What accounted for the generally negative attitude toward women, and what other steps did Jesus take throughout his ministry to counter that prejudice?

To learn more about Well Woman, see page 178.

Martha:

- Rational
- Responsible
- Practical
- Sturdy
- Persistant
- Forthright

Text: *John 11*

Setting: *Bethany (about two miles from Jerusalem), first century*

Significance: *Martha confronts Jesus after the death of her brother Lazarus and is overcome with joy when Lazarus is raised from the dead.*

Chapter 10

Martha of Bethany: Practical and Passionate

Grief had bitten into me like a wild dog, shaking me by the throat and refusing to let go. I wanted to throw up; I suppose it was to be expected. My brother Lazarus had died only four days earlier. He and my sister Mary and I were exceptionally close. It was always the three of us, but now death had interceded.

Keep the routines, I told myself. One step in front of the other. Make the beds. Sweep the courtyard. Water the herbs. Chop the vegetables.

It was the last action, the making of a simple meal, that I could not finish. The smell of leeks nauseated me. The knife seemed wobbly in my hand. My field of vision was like gravy at its edges.

Our guests and fellow mourners — there were dozens, in and out, in and out — would push me into a chair. "Martha, that's our job now. You need to grieve. That's why we're here. To help. Let go. Mourn. Grieve. Cry."

They were right. Friends and family took care of each other at a time like this. I must let them care for me for a change. I must try to eat, but all I could think of was Lazarus. It was impossible for me to sit still.

Death had come suddenly and we were unprepared. Is one ever prepared for the loss of a brother?

✠

Lazarus had taken ill and stumbled to bed, burning with fever. When he starting hallucinating, we sent a runner for our friend, Jesus.

We knew Jesus better than most people, for he and his friends often stayed with us when his work brought them near.

I kept the best linens fresh and clean, always ready for him. I harvested our garden within an inch of its life whenever he appeared, for he was always hungry. I prepared the most savory stews I knew and the most nourishing breads, always sending him off with extra loaves. We all took great delight in the laughter that filled the house when his friends crowded in.

Although he got the lame up and walking, often he could barely stand after a long day. Even though he gave the blind their sight, his eyes were sometimes bloodshot when he reached us, the power seemingly gone out of him. And although he inspired others with his eloquent talks, his voice was hoarse and tired late at night, requiring what seemed like gallons of black peppermint tea with honey to get it going again. That and a good night's sleep.

So I knew he could — and would — heal Lazarus. Was it not Jesus who had said that faith the size of a mustard seed could move a mountain? There was no problem there, for I had jars of mustard seeds.

I just needed him to show up.

✠

"Don't worry. Jesus is on his way. Everything will be all right," I told Lazarus, smoothing his matted hair.

Mary and I wiped his hot face with cool cloths and held saturated sponges to his lips, trying to will life back into his burning body, as he slept fitfully, fighting for air.

Late that afternoon I thought he was getting better, as his struggle lessened and his body seemed cooler. A brief smile emerged as he recognized us for the first time in days.

Yet like a breeze sneaks across a dark ocean, several hours later he slipped from our grasp without warning, without struggle. Slowly we realized that his chest was not moving. No breath warmed my face when I laid my cheek on his. His eyes were open, his jaw slack.

He was dead.

The next few hours were a blur as we witnessed Lazarus grow cold to the touch, saw his limbs stiffen. We washed and anointed him, wrapped him tightly and gave him over to the cool dark tomb.

✠

We grieved the loss of a brother gone far too early, but four days later, I had cried enough. Jesus had failed us. When I heard that he was finally approaching Bethany, I rushed to meet him while Mary remained at home with friends, staring into the empty hearth.

"Lord, if you had been here, my brother would not have died."
John 11:21

I didn't have to wait long. When Jesus walked toward me, he looked as tired and drawn as I'd ever seen him. In the old days I would have brought him to the house to rest, to eat. Now he got nothing but words from me.

"If you had been here, Lazarus would not have died."

I waited. No response.

"Even now," I said, "I know that God will give you whatever you ask."

Only then did his eyes meet mine.

"Your brother will rise again," he said.

"I know he will rise again," I said, "in the resurrection on the last day."

An almost imperceptible shake of his head met a growing lump in my throat.

"Martha, I am the resurrection and the life. Those who believe in me, even though they die, will live again. They are given eternal life because they believe in me and will never die. Do

"I am the resurrection and the life."
John 11:25

you believe that?"

"Yes, Lord," I said. "I believe. I believe that you are the Messiah, the Son of God, the one who is coming into the world."

This was not news to me. I had known his identity for some time. Still, a weight seemed to fall away from his shoulders. I could swear the corners of his mouth turned up, ever so slightly.

"Go get Mary. Please," he said.

I left. I loved Jesus and believed in him, but did not always understand him.

✠

Slipping into our house by the back door, I found Mary where I had left her, her eyes vacant.

"Mary," I whispered, "the Teacher is in town and is calling for you."

Rising without a word, she ran to meet Jesus. I was close on her heels.

When Jesus saw her weeping, and the Jews who came with her also weeping, he was greatly disturbed in spirit and deeply moved.
John 11:33

"Lord, if you had been here, my brother would not have died," she cried.

I had not told her what to say, yet our thoughts were the same.

In that moment, she could no longer hold in her grief. Sobbing, she fell at Jesus' feet, her body racked with sobs.

Something began to stir within him, for he, too, began to weep.

I still didn't understand, but I had never loved Jesus more.

Whispers were heard from the dozens of people who had ran from the house.

"He's given sight to the blind! Could not he have saved Lazarus?"

"He healed a dead girl in Capernaum! Why couldn't he do the same for their brother?"

"Let's see if he is who they say he is."

Jesus was practically carried upright to the tomb by the power of the crowd, pushing him along.

"Let's go see Lazarus," they chanted. "Let's go! Let's go!"

Upon reaching the tomb, my heart grieved. The stone was still tight against the entrance, just as we had left it.

"Push the rock aside," commanded Jesus.

"Lord, the smell!"

I couldn't believe the words coming out of my mouth.

The smell? The one person in the world who might be able to do something had arrived, and I was worried about the smell?

Decay set in quickly in our part of the world; that was why we were so careful to rub the body with spices and wrap it tightly. Lazarus would smell, for it had been four days. What sense did it make to drag the body out now? Surely Jesus knew what a dead man looked like. Much as I loved my brother, I did not want to see his corpse again.

Despite my plea, Jesus commanded the stone be rolled away.

Then he looked toward the sky.

"Abba, thank you for listening to me. You always hear me, but I'm talking out loud so that everyone here will know that you sent me."

"Daddy?"Abba meant Daddy. He was calling God "Daddy"?

Taking a deep breath, Jesus shouted in a voice that seemed as deep as the heavens: "Lazarus, COME OUT!"

Silence: dark, yawning silence from the tomb. We waited without making a sound, all focused on the gaping stillness, but there was nothing. Nothing but the silence that only exists in tombs: the silence of the dead. The absolute cold void of the dead.

Then...almost imperceptibly...a sound...a breath...a rattling...and a familiar shape bound in linen stumbled into the bright sunlight!

I could not believe what I was seeing. A dead man walking?

"Unbind him, and let him go."
John 11:44

"Unwrap him and let him go!" shouted Jesus.

Our beloved brother was alive.

We raced toward him, tearing off the strips in a frenzy. He had been in the deepest prison of all, death, and was now free.

Some of the mourners bolted, their faces white. But most of our friends and neighbors stayed, some glued to the ground, others jumping wildly in the air. Mary and I clung to Lazarus, afraid he would disappear should we let go. I had never known such joy.

Jesus said to her, "Did I not tell you that if you believed, you would see the glory of God?"
John 11:40

And Jesus smiled.

Why does Martha of Bethany matter today?

Resolute like none other, Martha stood steadfast in her belief that Jesus would have made a difference had he been there when Lazarus hung on the brink of death. Free enough to confront him in her practical and honest way, Martha acted. And Jesus heard. Such a relationship was based on the care and friendship that Martha had provided along the way — much like the myriad of tasks that many women do every day, including cooking, cleaning, and managing the home.

What learnings might Martha of Bethany inspire?

- It is easy to take this story for granted, given that Christians have believed in resurrection since Jesus overcame death, but raising someone from the dead — especially one who had been entombed for four days — was an unprecedented act. Think of someone you've loved who has died. Perhaps you witnessed the death, or saw the body in a casket. What would it be like to see that person resurrected and return to life?
- Determined and unwavering, Martha refused to let Jesus off the hook when it came to the death of her brother. What

does that say about her? What does it say about her faith? Do you think Jesus expected her request? How does she compare to the other women in this book?

- Jesus knew that Lazarus had died, but he did not hurry back to Bethany upon receiving Martha's request. Why might he have lingered?

To learn more about Martha of Bethany, see page 181.

Mary of Bethany:

- Contemplative
- Generous
- Unapologetic
- Passionate
- Loving

Text: *John 12, Luke 10*

Setting: *Bethany, first century*

Significance: *In a stunning act of personal generosity and prophetic wisdom, Mary pours scented oil on Jesus' feet, wipes them with her hair, and by doing so, lends him strength as he heads towards the Cross.*

Chapter 11

Mary of Bethany: Hospitality Extraordinaire

It was time
the talking had gone on
long enough

the men were clustered about
the One I loved
They listened
they nodded
they ate
they held forth
they took him for granted

they did not see
death marching toward him
swinging its cruel sword
soon to strike him down

Martha and I
had let the shadows fall
the night before
we talked
of how
this visit to Bethany
would be his last

his voice was
tired
scared

drained

they were taking from him
I wanted to give to him
a moment of pleasure
a minute of rest
a time of hope

the job of a woman
was to do this after death
not before
but he had made his decision
not to flee
he would go forward

I would stand with him
anointing him
preparing him
for what lay ahead
death

a year's worth of wages
had bought the oil
and now there
there was nothing to do but do it

I knelt by his feet
well-traveled, dirty, scarred feet
my tears fell
soon it would be over
this moment
his life

Pouring the oil on his feet

I rubbed it in
the softness
filling the cracks
the dirt disappearing

the life-giving scent
filling the room
announcing a change

they stopped talking
in the silence
with his eyes shut
a single tear escaped
with my hair
I coated every callus
joined his tear with mine
massaging the fatigue
from his bones
lifting for a minute
the grime of the earth
the battles, the miles, the pain
loosening the sorrow
his and mine

his feet were clean
his soul in reprieve
I hoped
with a memory of a moment
locked in

before the terror to come.

Mary of Bethany

If Jesus had ever wanted to get married, I would have been first in line, knocking down the door. There. I've said it. I loved him like there was no tomorrow. I could have spent the rest of my days with him and him alone and been the happiest woman in the world.

All he had to do was say, "Mary, come with me," and I would have left home and never turned back. But he had other things than marriage on his mind. Besides, that's not the way our lives worked. Girls were given in marriage by their fathers or brothers with nothing to say about it, often to a man who had more than one wife, often to a man who could treat you like dirt and you had no recourse. Love didn't matter; it was something that might come over time. Or not.

Truthfully, I don't know if Jesus ever thought about marriage. He had bigger things on his mind, and that made me love him even more.

Besides, he had friends. Turns out he'd already said, "Come with me," to twelve rugged, smelly, earthy, loud, boisterous men. Half of them fished for a living. One collected taxes. God knows what the others did. Jesus called them his disciples, and they followed him everywhere. To Galilee. To Capernaum. To Samaria. They were tan and strong and joyful and belligerent and they would have beat up anyone who tried to take him from their midst.

Jesus and his friends often stayed with us when passing through, and those were the happiest days of my life. And I did something that no one else did. It took all I had to do it, and it angered the disciples to no end.

✠

We lived together in the small town of Bethany: my sister Martha and I and our brother Lazarus. A widow, Martha had been left with a two-story house, built around a courtyard we shared with our neighbors. Most widows lost everything they had and were soon shuffled off to male relatives or had to prostitute themselves to provide scraps for the table.

But through the kindness of her former husband's family, and through the protection of Lazarus, Martha owned her own home and kept house for the three of us. When I say, "kept house," she kept it like God himself would be walking in the door any day. Swept no less than five times a day, the dirt floor was like satin. Curtains were lined up with precision like soldiers. Vegetables and herbs were nurtured as if they were babies, and grew trying to please their mother. Sleeping mats were brushed and hung in the sun to air each day. Soups and stews and bread beckoned to us like the best of friends.

One day I caught Martha gently shooing someone out the back door. I figured it to be our neighbor's child, Ezra, who was rewarded often at our home in his search for goodies, especially almond cookies and carob cake.

"Go," she was saying. "There you go. You should be out there, getting fresh air. Now take care of yourself."

Looking over her shoulder, I expected to see Ezra with his hands full, but no. Martha was on her hands and knees gently releasing a spider — a spider who apparently thought he might collar an errant bug in our home. I could have told him he'd find no bugs; the house was too clean. Nowhere else would a child, or a spider, for that matter, find a bigger heart than that which belonged to my sister.

✠

Martha's heart was matched only by that of Lazarus' ever-gregarious spirit. A carpenter by trade, he never came home alone; he had always made a new friend or two or three. It seemed that all the human odds and ends of Bethany and

Jerusalem found their way to our table at one point or another. Was it that he roamed the streets looking for new friends? Or did he find them through his work of building houses and benches and tables, always telling people what they needed, always interacting. Both, I figured.

He held court in our small home almost nightly, but it was a different kind of court, with all present laughing, telling stories, eating their fill of cheese, fish, bread, vegetables and nuts. Light from our oil lamps would often spill onto the street and into our courtyard until the early morning hours, punctuated by sounds from lyres and tambourines.

We knew we were blessed with friends and music and song. Yet I did not know how much until my brother showed up one afternoon with Jesus. And his friends.

Coming in from the front door, Lazarus heard us talking in the courtyard out back, shielded from the broiling sun by colorful tarps we had woven, dyed in different shades of lavender. Drinking cool water laced with pomegranate berries and mint, we were recounting the events of the night before, when he had brought home a few girls of unconventional means. Even Martha had been amused, but truly happy when they had gone home.

He poked his head out the back door.

"Hello, girls. I'm starved. Lots of work today, with that windstorm last week. Anything cooking for dinner?"

The answer was yes, of course, for when had it ever been no? Since when did he ask?

I guess Martha thought she'd have a little fun that day. "Laz, do you ever stop eating?" she mumbled, her eyes closed as if deep in sleep. "I thought we'd take a break from food today."

"Oh. Reeaaallly?"

"Yes, I thought I'd just sit here for the rest of the day. Maybe the evening. Maybe my whole life."

My eyes widened. This was unlike Martha. What was she

saying? What was she thinking?

Behind Lazarus, I could see the whole room was packed. Hot sweaty men filled the place, their work-a-day clothes mostly in tatters, their faces red from the sun. I could just imagine he'd told his new friends that his house had the best food in the world and the most welcoming sisters. "Martha," I whispered. "You might want to open your eyes."

"I think I'll rest a little longer."

With that, the woman starting snoring.

"MARTHA!" I hissed. "WAKE UP!"

"That's okay. Let her rest. She must need it. She's barely slept since Josiah died."

Josiah? What was this about Josiah, her beloved husband? Who would know that she couldn't sleep? I alone knew that she was starved for sleep; she tossed for hours in her bed each night, finally finding slumber through whispered prayers and psalms, but still getting up each morning exhausted. I never spoke of it. Neither did she.

✠

The speaker edged his way into the courtyard. Unlike the others — none of them heavy, although almost all looked sturdy and broad-shouldered — he was tall, smooth of complexion, with long fingers and toes. And slender. Exceedingly slender. The rope around his waist was wrapped four times. Had my sister seen his frame, she would have been lobbing food at him in hopes of keeping him alive.

Women in our time were supposed to keep their eyes to themselves, to not make direct eye contact with men, especially strange ones. Yet I had a feeling that this man was no stranger. My eyes roved from his feet to his eyes and back again.

Caked with dirt, his feet looked like they had walked hundreds of miles without seeing water or a wash rag. The strap of one sandal was torn and had been replaced with rope; the sole of the other looked like a piece of parchment between his foot and the floor.

It was his eyes, though, that held my attention. I found myself talking to them with my own. Talking? How can you talk with your eyes?

Later I would learn that those very eyes had seen the darkness separate from light at creation as God's spirit brooded over the nothingness that would soon be the earth. I would learn that with one fling of his hand, the stars and planets cascaded into motion. The reason he didn't feel like a stranger was because he wasn't; he'd been with me all along, even as I came into being in my mother's womb.

I knew none of that then. All I knew was that I never wanted this man to leave.

✠

"Martha, don't worry about food for us," Jesus said, his voice lilting with a slight Galilean accent. "It's good for you to rest, for your busywork satisfies that empty place in your heart. You give so much to others already that we cannot ask anymore. Embracing others is one of your true gifts. Yet even a heart needs rest. Yours does."

Even a heart needs rest? Who was this man?

"Martha, Mary, this is Jesus," said Lazarus, edging his way into the courtyard. "And his friends: Peter, Thomas, John, James, Andrew, Bartholomew, ah...that's enough for now. Welcome, everyone. Welcome!"

With that, Martha flew into action like a dog scattering doves on the town square. I, on the other hand, moved slowly. Very slowly. All I wanted to do was sit and hear what the man had to say, and that's pretty much what I did for the next three hours. I didn't move.

Jesus talked about God. About healing. About something called redemption. Mostly he told stories: about fishing and collecting coins and keeping lamps lit and sowing seeds. Some didn't make sense, but most did. I could have listened to him for hours. And I did.

✠

"Martha, I'll help you," I stammered at one point, aware that my sister was working alone to make a huge meal. But I wasn't going anywhere. I didn't move.

Martha, on the other hand, was like a five-man army. She went for one of her favorites for supper: rack of lamb with spicy mint sauce. I don't know what got into her, for such a meal was usually only for celebrations like weddings, but I let her have at it, alone. Like a spinning top that children throw, she ran to the butcher, clipped the herbs, simmered the sauce, mixed in the honey and set the table.

As time went on, there was an increasing clatter between the corner kitchen and the courtyard where our hearth was located. Still, I did not move.

Finally red-faced and perspiring, Martha stumbled into the room. Individual conversations were going on between Peter and James and Andrew over in the corner about fishing. John and I and Matthew and three of the other disciples were clustered around Jesus, all sitting on the floor, waiting for his next words.

She stood behind us for a minute, too polite to interrupt. Then she spoke words that hung in the air like an imminent storm.

"If you all want to eat, I can't do it alone. Jesus, tell Mary to help me."

Some would have thought she was complaining. Maybe she was. She deserved to. She had cooked dinner for fifteen of us single-handedly.

"Martha," Jesus said quietly. "Mary has chosen the better part."

I have chosen the better part? Reeeally.

I looked at her, wide-eyed.

Martha, bless her heart, began to smile. Then she sat beside me, breathed deeply, and put her head on my shoulder.

She was still, finally still. He had somehow calmed her spirit. When she rose to finish making dinner, I went with her. Later that night, I noticed that she was no longer sleeping fitfully; she slept peacefully that night and for the years to come.

✠

From then on, Jesus and his friends visited every few months. We would never know exactly when they were coming, although town boys would often run ahead with the news.

My favorite visits were the times he would show up unannounced. Soon the street out front and the courtyard would be packed. Faces would peek in the windows. Villagers would stand on nearby rooftops, hoping to get a glimpse of him.

Once or twice, later on, they all came after dark. I knew it was because his days were full, but wondered if it was also because they could slip into town more easily. His slim frame was increasingly more gaunt, his feet blistered and worn.

At least for a time, Jesus seemed to lay his troubles aside at our home. I finally realized he wasn't coming just for meals, or for a place to sleep. His soul was fed as much as ours, and it was our honor to give him a place to lay his head.

✠

The last time we saw Jesus he entered Bethany late in the afternoon. We hadn't seen him since he had raised Lazarus from the dead. Yes, our brother Lazarus. That was something none of us had expected...a miracle true. Because of it, and because he was seen as a troublemaker, the authorities were looking for him.

Raising Lazarus had been the act that pushed things over the edge. He was now a wanted man; the chief priests and Pharisees had put out the word that he was to be arrested on sight.

I knew I should listen to his words, for it might be the last time I would hear them. But for that one time, I couldn't. His feet drew my attention like bees to nectar. I could not keep my eyes from them. They looked like they could not walk one more mile. Normally a host would kneel down, pull a towel off his shoulder and wash a guest's feet upon greeting him by the door. Lazarus had forgotten.

The more I stared at his feet, I knew I wanted to make things right.

Martha only had the house; she didn't have any money. Neither did I. But Lazarus was a saver. I slipped up to the roof, in the corner where he slept, and moved a stack of bricks. Grabbing the gold coins that he had saved over the years, I ran to the village square where a merchant kept a tent filled with apothecary goods. In my hands was money that would take a year to earn. I prayed Lazarus would forgive me.

The merchant had a bottle of nard on his top shelf; the whole town knew it. From the East, it was fit for a king. We had few kings passing through, so we thought he was crazy to keep it.

"The nard," I said. "Give me the nard."

The man rolled his eyes, then locked them on my chest. I was a woman on the streets, late in the day, without a male escort, forbidden to be alone.

"Maybe I should give you a coin or two," he said. "You know, money that you can really earn. For pleasing me."

"Give me the nard, now!" I barked, throwing the coins down on the counter.

He complied. As I walked away, his jaw remained slack; his eyes locked on the money that would soon roll across his sweaty palms.

✠

Clasping the nard to my chest like it was a baby, I ran down the hill to our house, caring only that it arrived safely. Sated, the disciples sat around Jesus as he talked of God, of prayer, of better things to come. For once, I didn't care what he was saying, and I didn't care what the others thought. All I knew was that I was going to use the oil for the purpose it had been made — to anoint a king. And yes, to prepare that king for the coming days. Most likely, for his death.

Mary took a pound of costly perfume made of pure nard, anointed Jesus' feet, and wiped them with her hair.
John 12:3

Breathe. In, out. In, out.

All conversation stopped behind me as I knelt by Jesus' feet. Off came his sandals, out came the cork. The aroma filled the house: clean, deep, evocative, sensual, calling us out of our senses — calling us to something higher, better, more than we were on our own.

Tears dropped from my eyes onto his feet. When I reached for a towel to wipe both his feet and my face, there was none. I had forgotten to put one over my shoulder in the time-honored way hosts do.

So I used the closest thing: my hair. Carefully, gently, completely, my hair became the towel as I wiped the oil from every inch of Jesus' feet.

Never had I done something so carefully. Never had I done something so holy. Never had I loved so much.

Judas Iscariot, one of the disciples (he who was to betray him), said, "Why was this ointment not sold for three hundred denarii and given to the poor?"
John 12:4

Leaning back on my heels as I finished, I could hear belligerent voices behind me.

"What does she think she's doing?"

"Lazarus, get your sister out of here! She has no right to touch him like that!"

"That smell is too much! It's like a bordello in here!"

"No, it smells like a palace! Of kings and princes!"

Then one caustic voice rose by itself, filled with anger: "Why was this ointment not sold for three hundred denarii and given to the poor?!"

I knew that voice, foaming with self-righteousness: it belonged to Judas.

"You always have the poor with you, but you do not always have me." John 12:8

Judas, the one who would sell our Lord to the devil in only a few days, was commiserating about the poor. The poor! Never had he expressed an authentic interest in them. As the self-appointed treasurer for the group, he counted coins daily, yet no one had believed that he had given them to the needy.

"Let her alone, let her keep it for the day of my burial! The poor you always have with you, but you do not always have me. She has done well by me!"

"Leave her alone. She bought it so that she might keep it for the day of my burial." John 12:7

Stupefied, the disciples fell silent. Jesus himself had come to my rescue. My Lord and brother, my friend and soulmate had reached out and pulled me further into his heart, protecting me from those who would humiliate me. Nothing else mattered.

Why does Mary of Bethany matter today?

Mary of Bethany ministered to Jesus in a human and eloquent way — a way that angered the disciples and left them highly uncomfortable, because of her "out-of-the-box" style. Jesus treasured Mary because she sought to understand his teachings and before all others, she affirmed his choice to go toward Jerusalem, toward the way of the cross, toward the authorities who would end his life. She did not try to control his actions or mourn them prematurely; she lent her love and support.

What learnings might Mary inspire?

- Make no mistake: the act of a woman pouring luxurious scented oil onto a man's feet and then drying them with her hair is a sensual act. How did this action help prepare Jesus for death?
- Why were the disciples angry over Mary's behavior? Were they justified or not?
- Mary and Martha embodied the ministry of hospitality in their relationship with Jesus. Martha always had a meal and a fresh bed ready for him while Mary was a constant listener. What can be learned from their actions?

To learn more about Mary of Bethany, see page 183.

Mary Magdalene:

- Bold
- Committed
- Loyal
- Unpretentious
- Fearless

Text: *John 20, Luke 8*

Setting: *Jerusalem, first century*

Significance: *Mary Magdalene is the first to see the risen Jesus and, according to John's Gospel, the first to tell the others the good news.*

Chapter 12

Mary Magdalene: Forever Changed

I hadn't slept. Not that it mattered. Not that much of anything mattered anymore. My best friend was dead.

Perhaps that's why I didn't care that we were in danger ourselves, rushing through the chilly, dark streets of Jerusalem so early that morning. But we could not wait any longer. It had been grueling to get through the Sabbath knowing we could not touch Jesus. Now we were finally free to begin our work of anointing him, wrapping him in fresh linen and sealing him into the dark tomb. Forever.

His death was finally starting to sink in. We never thought it would happen. Although he had told us that it was approaching, I had never believed him.

Shaking, Mary and Salome and I and the others had stood at Golgotha as we watched him die, parched and broken. We cringed as they jabbed vinegar to his lips when all he wanted was water. We cursed the ravens as they gathered, hungrily, after the blood poured from his side. I wanted nothing more than to rush the cross, pull him down, carry him to safety.

And I would have, only his eyes told me to hold my ground. He knew I would have risked all for him.

Unlike the others, I was not afraid of suffering, for torture had taught me well in my early years. My body was my prison; I was locked inside with seven demons patrolling every corner of me. I knew they would kill me in the end after they finished sucking out whatever joy and sanity was left.

Perhaps one would chase me to my death — or perhaps another would force me to hurt someone and I would be stoned. Or maybe they would continue to steal what little spirit I had left, seducing me further down the trail of despair.

✠

By the time I met Jesus, I had almost given up. Try as I did, fear greeted my every move; isolation ruled each encounter.

Yet in a private moment, with a simple touch, he healed me: mind, body and spirit. He seemed to know my very being before he laid hands on me. And he knew the demons as well, even calling all seven by name.

"Leave her alone," he said. "The woman will be free."

The woman will be free.

For the first time in my life, I was healthy. My mind was clear of the horrible weights that had burdened me for so long. I could trust myself and for the first time, others could trust me, too.

I had friends: his friends, now mine as well. The women were like sisters and I guarded them with my heart and soul. The men were kind and respectful, a new experience. Barriers began to fall. Laughter was a new gift, generosity a lifestyle.

And I had purpose. For I was coming to know the soul of God.

I had stood there at the cross, watching every jagged breath until there were no more. Near the end he couldn't lift his face to see us. I finally let my tears flow, knees buckling to the ground. Then he was gone, ripped away, my Sun blocked, all hope destroyed.

✠

And so we walked to his grave.

Deep breath, deep breath. One foot in front of the other, eyes straight ahead.

The huge rock that the guards had set in place would be tight against the entrance; I hoped we had the strength to move it ourselves.

But as we rounded the corner, my heart jerked like a dove on the chopping block. No! NO!

The rock was gone. Darkness loomed from the hole. Mary screamed; I dropped the flask holding the death spices.

My old demons would have pushed me into the hole. But thanks to them, I knew about darkness; I knew I would survive and come out. Holding Mary's lamp with shaking hands, I pushed in.

Save for scattered burial clothes, the tomb was empty.

First they had killed him; now they had stolen his body.

Damn those disciples. They needed to be here. Now.

I turned and ran to Simon Peter's house. If anyone could do anything, it would be Peter. I knew he would be furious. I could count on him to jump in and make things right.

His house was dark when I arrived, just like the early morning sky. Pounding on the front door, I yelled as loud as I could. I must have looked the mad woman I used to be. I didn't care.

"Open up! Open up!"

It seemed like ages before the door creaked open. And once it did, I stood stunned. Peter looked as bone-tired as I'd ever seen him. Deep circles under his eyes underscored a pale and scared face. Peter scared? Peter tired?

The man had the energy of fifteen. He was like a bull. He was always Peter — loud, boisterous, impulsive, clumsy Peter. But there was no spirit to him that morning. Like a hunted man, he glanced up and down the street, and then pulled me in. He must have thought I was a Roman soldier when he first heard my knock.

"They have stolen him out of the tomb and I do not know where he is!"

That was all it took for the man I knew to emerge. He took off running with John, who had been spending the night at his home, hiding from the soldiers. John,

"They have taken the Lord out of the tomb, and we do not know where they have laid him."
John 20:13b

younger and quicker, reached the tomb first. But seconds later, Peter arrived, with me on his heels. Taking charge, he pushed the younger man out of the way.

Like it had me, darkness enveloped him. Peter backed out of the small space, shaking his head. For once, he had nothing to say and walked away, empty in both spirit and expression. John and the women followed, heads down.

✠

I had nowhere to go. Leaning against the rocks of the tomb, I tried to figure out what to do next. Go after the other disciples? Look in other tombs? Perhaps the others were right. Maybe it was time to go home, to say goodbye to Jesus for good.

Mary stood weeping outside the tomb, and as she wept she stooped to look into the tomb; and she saw two angels in white, sitting where the body of Jesus had lain, one at the head and one at the feet."
John 20:11-12

No. I would not give up. He deserved more from me. I would not abandon him.

I stooped down, peering in one more time. As my eyes grew adjusted, I could see two angels, wrapped in white, sitting on the rock ledge, about six feet apart, where his body had lain!

"Why are you crying?" asked one.

"Because they have taken my Lord away and I do not know where they have put him!"

And with that, I felt someone behind me.

"Woman, why are you weeping?"
John 20:13a

Again the same question. The same stupid question from this, the gardener.

"Why are you crying?"

Had these people made up their minds to torture me or was it just spontaneous? How many times did I have to say the same thing?

Enough!

"Sir," I said. "Just tell me where he is and I will go get him." Just tell me so that I can give his godforsaken body some peace. Just tell me so at least I can end this nightmare.

"Mary."

That voice. I knew that voice.

"Mary."

Could it be? No. It couldn't. I had seen too much not to be a realist. I had been disappointed too many times.

But his eyes gave it away. They seemed to start a smile that would not stop.

Supposing Jesus to be the gardener, she said to him, "Sir, if you have carried him away, tell me where you have laid him, and I will take him away."
John 20:15

Then I remembered. He said he would rise from the dead in three days, and here he was!

"Rabbouni," I screamed, "Rabbouni!"

✠

As I rushed toward him, he put up his hand.

"Don't cling to me, Mary."

Cling? Cling?

Like the soldier's spear piercing Jesus' side, the word stabbed my heart.

I wanted so badly to hug him and not let him go, ever.

"I haven't yet ascended to my Father. Go and tell my brothers that I am joining my father and your father, my God and your God."

Go and tell my brothers.

Time seemed suspended, almost like the day when he had breathed his last. Only then the sky thundered, almost breaking in two. Now I could swear there was laughter from the

Mary Magdalene went and announced to the disciples, "I have seen the Lord"; and she told them that he had said these things to her.
John 20:18

clouds, an energy that was like a thousand angel wings beating with joy.

My heart was unbearably full. I would do what he asked.

Why does Mary Magdalene matter today?

Jesus loves us deeply and wants to heal us from both the pain of life's tragedies and the burden of sin. Mary Magdalene led the journey to Jesus' dark tomb expecting the worst, but wanting to care for her friend until the very end. Perhaps the courage behind that action was made possible by her own journey with mental illness from which Jesus had cured her. Complete healing was found for Mary as Jesus chose her for his first resurrection appearance.

What learnings might Mary Magdalene inspire?

- Although the Gospels vary slightly about who was present at the empty tomb, they all agree on this point: women were the first to see the risen Christ. Why might have Jesus have appeared first to them?
- In John's Gospel, Mary Magdalene was the first to see him after the resurrection. Such an action denotes a close and trusting relationship. Why wouldn't he let her touch him?
- Put yourself in Mary Magdalene's shoes, or sandals, if you will. What would it have been like to be present at the tomb on the day that Jesus changed the world forever?

To learn more about Mary Magdalene, see page 185.

Epilogue

Friends ask piercing questions at times, and that certainly happened in the writing and sharing of this book. Why were women treated so badly over the centuries? What happened to those people that died so that Jewish and/or Christian people might live?

The answers begin with the scarlet cord. Rahab anchored the cord from her window so that she and her family might be saved. But that action sprang from faith — Rahab believed in a God who was larger than she, in a God who protected his people, in a God who would light the way from the darkness in which she lived.

The cord was not just a piece of rope; rather, it was a connection to a better life, a statement of faith, of trust, of the future. By hanging the cord, Rahab helped God's people cross into the Promised Land.

And what about those people of Jericho, and their cattle, who were put to death by the Hebrews? What about the Canannites who lay slain on the battlefield after the war with Barak and Deborah? What about those innocent children who were slaughtered by Pharaoh just after Jesus escaped to Egypt?

There is no end to pain and suffering in this world. Yet, as with life, God also intercedes in death — comforting the sorrowful, extending a hand. The choice to respond is always ours, even *after* death.

Throwing out the cord was an invitation for healing by Rahab. Once she did that, God saw, God listened, God acted. In that action between God and woman, and through the other stories that make up this book, God offers us hope. Whether we are stricken with cancer or lose a loved one or are starving ourselves, God is present. It is up to us to throw out the scarlet cord and ask for healing, ask for redemption, ask for reconciliation.

These narratives are meant to give us hope and to raise up those who will not know the full presence of God's healing until after death.

So, here is to Rahab and all the forgotten women of the Bible...and those women who are raped or killed in Kenya or the Congo and tossed aside like trash. For you this book is written as a sign of hope, a sign that you will not be forgotten, that there is a God who cares and who stands ready to embrace you, that your sacrifices and life choices mean something long after you are gone, and that your life does make a full and holy difference.

Learn More

Learn more about Rahab

Rahab is only one of two women (Sarah was the other) named in the New Testament's Letter to the Hebrews as a hero of the faith. "By faith Rahab the harlot did not perish with those who were disobedient, because she had given friendly welcome to the spies." (Hebrews 11:31)

To this day, there exists debate among scholars regarding the man whom Rahab married. Jewish tradition points to Rahab marrying Joshua, Moses' successor. However, Matthew's genealogy of Jesus (Matthew 1:5) lists Rahab as the wife of Salmon, who well could have been one of the spies that she sheltered. Either way, she is named as an ancestor of Jesus. Given her occupation as a prostitute and her initial status as a person outside the Jewish faith, she is a fairly colorful addition to Jesus' lineage.

Located between the double walls of Jericho, Rahab's house measured about twelve by fifteen feet.[3] There were most likely two floors, with a rooftop that afforded both living and working space, necessary in a warm climate with no air-conditioning or modern conveniences.

Hebrew Bible scholar Tikva Frymer-Kensky draws a parallel of Rahab's actions with those of Passover, both being marked in red, the former from the window and the latter from the door post. "The alert reader...may catch the reference. On the night of the slaying of the firstborn of Egypt, the Israelites marked their doors with lamb's blood and stayed inside. Rahab's family, inside the house marked in red, is to be rescued from Jericho as the Israelites were from Egypt."[4]

After forty years in the wilderness, the Israelites emerged a strong and cohesive nation. Part of what they had learned in that process was the nature of warfare, both defense and self-protection. Another was the maturing of the promise that God had given Abraham and Sarah — the promise of land and descendants. As Jericho was the first city inside that land, its residents faced a deadly prospect: obliteration. Rahab alone seemed to understand that risk.

In her book, *Women in the Old Testament,* author Irene Nowell explores the tradition of Holy War, and the custom of *herem* operative in the destruction of Jericho: no prisoners taken, all material things destroyed.[5] The Bible confirms that all living things were killed — men and women, young and old, even the animals.

For Rahab's story: Joshua 2:1-22, 6:1-7, 20-25

Learn More about Eve

The Book of Genesis (3:1) identifies the serpent as the "most crafty figure in the garden." History has always assumed the male voice for the great tempter, but who is to say what form or gender it took? One thing is sure: like a child molester, the serpent would have presented itself as trustworthy, reliable and, no doubt, attractive. Made in God's image, Eve was an intelligent woman. Chances are few that she would have taken the one thing that God had forbidden in a spontaneous interaction from a random serpent.

The words "I AM," which end the poem, are well-known in the Bible. Spoken by God to describe himself as he urged Moses to plead with Pharaoh to free the Israelites, he said, "Just tell them that "I AM has sent me to you," (Exodus 3:14). By referring to himself as "I AM," God summed up both past and future, stating his place in history as Alpha and Omega, beginning and end.
By exercising her own free will, even though that option involved

sin, Eve too came to terms with all of who she was — her own "I AM" — assuming a unique role in human history. She began to know the consequences of choosing evil over good. Sadly, that experience distanced her from God.

For an initial understanding of Eve, think modern teenager: pushing against boundaries, challenging those things — and sometimes only those things — that parents hold as essential values to keep their children safe. Teenagers grow up, and so did Eve and Adam. In *Listen to Her Voice,* Author Miki Raver explores how Eve's action was evidence that God had given human beings free will, and that her dilemma was a choice between a safety and passive acceptance or a knowledge-based act involving independence and risk.[6]

The big question: Why did God set the Tree in the garden? Some would say it was to test Adam and Eve. Others see it as God providing an option for Adam and Eve to grow up, move out on their own, and become fully human. Author Naomi Rosenblatt concludes that it was only after leaving the Garden that Adam and Eve entered into a sexual relationship and became parents. Given that Genesis points out that Adam and Eve "knew" each other after leaving the Garden, but does not mention a sexual relationship before their departure, that question remains open.

Where was Eden? Scholars are in disagreement over this, for of the four rivers mentioned in the Bible that flowed from the garden (Pison, Gihon, Tigris and Euphrates), two no longer exist. In the last hundred years, eastern Turkey was seen as the most viable site; however, an emerging and quite plausible theory suggests that the Garden of Eden may have existed under the present site of the Persian Gulf.[7]

For Eve's story: Genesis 3:1-4:16

Learn more about Sarah

Love was not a prerequisite for marriage in Sarah's time, and it was rarely the reason why people married. Most marriages were arranged for economic or cultural reasons, and some men, especially wealthy ones, had more than one wife. But despite their ups and downs, Sarah's and Abraham's story is one of the great love stories of all time and reminds the modern reader of many contemporary challenges in marriage, including infidelity, power struggles, infertility and the search for a lasting home.

In ancient Israel infertility was considered both a tragedy and a curse. Those without children had nothing to pass on to future generations and their existence on earth was like a passing thought, brief and fleeting. While Sarah's action of initiating a sexual relationship between Hagar and Abraham might seem strange or offensive to the modern reader, several things must be observed: Sarah had waited many long years to become pregnant; she may have thought she was assisting God in his promise (see next note); and she refused to surrender the hope of giving birth to her own son.

Abraham had sexual intercourse with Hagar at Sarah's suggestion because children born from such a surrogate relationship would be considered his and Sarah's (this understanding had its roots beginning with the Code of Hammurabi, eighteenth century BC).[8] Thus, God's promise of "as many ancestors as there were stars in the sky" would be fulfilled.

As Sarah's servant, Hagar had no choice about whether she would have sex with Abraham once it had been decreed by Sarah. Cultural mores were different then; it was not unusual for men to have more than one wife; and the Bible, although not all translations, says that Sarah gave [Hagar] to Abraham as a wife (Genesis 16.3) Under the circumstances, perhaps she was eager to give birth to his child; perhaps not. Regardless of marital status, bearing Abraham's heir would raise her social status. Still, it is impossible to know what Hagar thought or felt about the whole situation.

Like Sarah and Abraham, Hagar finds redemption. Even though she suffered greatly, God protected both Hagar and Ishmael and led them to safety. Ishmael is thought to be the progenitor of Islam. Later references in the Bible indicate that Abraham visited Ishmael; the Koran also references an ongoing relationship between father and son. Scholar Irene Nowell points out that Hagar is the sole person in the Bible to confer God with a name, saying "You are the God of Vision." (Genesis 16:13) [9]

God, through his angels, interacts with Hagar in a deep and dynamic way. As Rabbi Joseph Telushkin notes in *Biblical Literacy: The Most Important People, Events and Ideas of the Hebrew Bible,* the first time a messenger of God speaks to a woman, he chooses a non-Hebrew, a woman who is low in social standing in her own culture, and significantly, one that will become "the mother of another religion!"[10]

Much is made of Sarah's reaction to Abraham's infidelity, even though it was her idea. However, Sarah may also have stepped outside the bonds of marriage during their desert travels, as she was taken into a harem of a local king at Abraham's suggestion (Genesis 20:2). The action was designed to save their lives while traveling through the desert. While it is unclear if a sexual relationship occurred between the king and Sarah, Abraham passed Sarah off as his sister (which may have been technically true, as children often had the same fathers but different mothers in extended family clans).

Sarah and Abraham's journey toward the Promised Land was

one of great significance, as it symbolizes the very beginnings of not only the Judeo/Christian tradition, but also the search for a permanent home granted by God. The Promised Land is of course modern-day Israel, and is only the second land that has been specifically provided by God — the first being the Garden of Eden.

Although Abraham spent much of his life traveling toward the Promised Land, he never lived there; but he did buy a piece of property in which to bury Sarah when she died at the age of 127 (the cave of Machpelah, near Mamre; Genesis 23:19). Isaac and Ishmael reunited to bury Abraham there (Genesis 25:9) when he died at the age of 175; several succeeding generations were buried there as well.

As the text indicates, God changed Sarah's and Abraham's names, ever so slightly, to declare their changed identities. This is not unusual in the Bible once individuals have entered into life-changing covenants with God or Jesus (e.g., Isaac's name was changed to Jacob and Saul to Paul).

For Sarah's story: Genesis 12:1-20, 15:1-6, 16:1-6, 17:51-21, 18:1-15, 20:1-21:10, 23:1-2
For Hagar's story: Genesis 16:7-16, 21:7-20

Learn more about Deborah

Deborah's story is found in the Book of Judges, a rather gruesome chronicle spanning 325 years of the Hebrew people's initial troubled history in the Promised Land. Her goal, like the other leaders who arose during that time, was to free the Israelites from oppression and restore allegiance to God and God alone. Upon a careful study of Judges, the reader may be stunned or angered to discover the level of brutality present — e.g., the killing of every Canaanite soldier in the battle at Mount Tabor. The reader may also remember the city of Jericho falling to the Israelites where all living things were killed except Rahab and her family.

How best to reconcile such brutality, especially since God continually raises up leaders in Judges to defeat the enemy and seems pleased when all is destroyed? Is the God of the Old Testament different from that of the New? Classic Christian theology would say that God is changeless. What is clear is this: God works through all situations for good, and is on the side of oppressed peoples throughout the Bible. This epic tale sustained the Jewish people through centuries of exile.

As prophet, judge and leader, Deborah holds a singular place in history. Rabbi Joseph Telushkin states that although she may be regarded as "a biblical Joan of Arc,"[11] (who lived in France more than 2000 years later and was burned at the stake). Deborah's life apparently continued in peace after the conquest at Mount Tabor, and Israel lived in peace for forty years.

Consider the meaning of these names, especially in the context of Deborah's story. In Hebrew, the name Barak means "lightening flash"; while several commentators translate Deborah's name, "eshet lapidot," as "woman of flames." Explosive power, indeed!

One may also be surprised to read the account of Jael's murder of Sisera in the Bible, as it ranges far beyond normal Sunday School fare. While she is not the only woman in the Bible to commit murder, the circumstances seem particularly brutal. However, war is war, and significantly, the poet of Judges 5 holds her in high esteem, calling her "most blessed of women," (Judges 5:24) for she killed an oppressor and potential rapist.

How exactly was it that Jael was able to have the fatal encounter with Sisera? Since women were in charge of pitching tents, Jael would have had the tent peg handy. Since men were not allowed in women's tents, no one would have thought to look for Sisera there. Jael's husband Heber was a Kenite, and Kenites were often itinerant iron workers. Separating himself from his clan before the battle (Judges 4:11) may have indicated his desire to be close to the Canaanites should their chariots or other equipment need repair.[12] Either way, Jael would have been near the battle.

Like the other women in this book, both Deborah and Jael showed initiative, the latter literally taking matters into her own hands. Like many of the women in the Bible, they are in partnership, friendly or not, bringing God's work to fruition. Consider Rachel and Leah, Mary and Martha, Sarah and Hagar. Two are better than one; often God provides allies and friends along the way.

As in so many stories in the Hebrew Bible and the New Testament, water takes on a key role, one that symbolizes freedom. As God caused the Kishon River to flood, the Canaanite warriors floundered, leaving themselves open to attack. This story also calls to mind the crossing of the Jordan River by Rahab and her newly found Hebrew community, and the placing of Moses in the Nile River to save his life from a bloodthirsty Pharaoh. Such images of freedom and new life are, for the Christian, ultimately celebrated in the waters of baptism.

For Deborah's story: Judges 4:1-16; Deborah's Song: Judges 5:1-31
For Jael's story: Judges 4:17-23, 5:24-27

Learn more about Hannah

Imagine Hannah's joy upon learning she was pregnant after so many years of infertility. And then consider the strength it took to give up little Samuel. It is hard enough to set free a young man or woman who has reached adulthood; it is another thing, and considerably much harder, to walk away from a toddler. Hannah's sacrifice is reminiscent of Abraham's in that both Hannah and Abraham offer God the one thing that brings more delight to their lives than anything: their sons. Abraham thought that God was asking him to slay his son, while Hannah trusted that Samuel would be raised to serve God. Still the similarity is striking: parents who put God's interests ahead of their own.

Although there are a number of other mother/young son stories in the Bible (Moses and his mother, Jochebed; Sarah and Isaac; John the Baptist and Elizabeth; Jesus and Mary, etc.) Hannah is the only woman to actively seek out God and negotiate with him in search of her heart's greatest desire: a child.

Hannah is also the first person in the Bible to visit a shrine to engage in private prayer. The modern reader might take her action for granted — that of directly talking to God on sacred ground. However, in those days, people came to the temple for two things: to offer a sacrifice of an animal in place of one's sins, or to engage in public worship. Hannah changed that equation, sharing her troubles with God, and God richly blessed her.

The temple at Shiloh, the place where Hannah prayed and Samuel grew up, housed the Ark of the Covenant. Believing that the ark signified God's abiding presence, the Hebrew people carried this treasure with them in war and in peace until it finally resided in the temple built by Solomon at Jerusalem. Inside the ark — the location of which is now a mystery — resided the two stone tablets upon which the Ten Commandments were written as well as a golden urn holding ancient manna and Aaron's rod.

When Hannah brings Samuel back to Eli, she is not full, at least outwardly, of sorrow. Rather, she utters what has become known as the Song of Hannah (see Samuel 2:1-10), a rich proclamation of God's raising up of the lowly over those who torment them. This song is a forerunner of the words that poured forth from Mary upon learning that she would give birth to Jesus (Luke 1:46-55).

Scholar Richard Bauckham, among others, notes that while both Hannah and Mary give thanks to God for their sons, they also celebrate God's active hand in delivering Israel from centuries of oppression. "As in Hannah's case, so in Mary's, her motherhood will lead to the salvation of Israel by her son, salvation that characteristically reverses the status of the lowly and the exalted. In her humiliation as a barren wife, Hannah is representative of oppressed Israel, whose liberation her son will achieve..." [13]

Why was Samuel so important to Israel? Since the time of Moses and Joshua, some two hundred years earlier, there had been no central figure to unite the Hebrew people. A series of brutal rulers had dominated them, and the strength and unity achieved during their forty years in the wilderness had dissipated. As priest, prophet and judge, Samuel helped spiritually reunite the twelve tribes of Israel into one nation and found and anointed the first two kings of Israel: Saul and David.

For Hannah's story: 1 Samuel 1:1-28, 2:18-21; Hannah's Prayer: 1 Samuel 2:1-10

Learn more about Ruth

This is a story of faith, vulnerability, honor and romance. It also symbolizes the depth of God's breakthrough miracles on both personal and national levels, as Ruth was a Moabite — a group particularly hated by the Israelites (see next page) and a woman encircled by death on all sides: her husband, her brother-in-law, and her father-in-law. Through the emotional pain that Ruth endured and the fidelity she maintained with her first husband's family, one more building block was put in place for two key events: the births of the boy, David, who would grow to be king, and that of Jesus, the Son of God.

Hesed is a Jewish word for sacred kindness, based on the covenant between God and his people, and this story is filled with characters who practice *hesed*. Naomi wanted the best for Ruth and Orpah as she ordered them back to their families in Moab; Ruth sacrificed ties with her own family to accompany Naomi; and Boaz cared for Ruth from the first day in the fields, because she had treated Naomi so well. God rewards them richly.

It is easy to take Ruth and Naomi's actions for granted in these days of cell phones, e-mail, and relatively safe travel. Consider this: when they set out for Bethlehem, Ruth was completely severing ties with her own family and both were entering an unknown and potentially dangerous situation. Although Bethlehem was only forty miles from Moab, there were no police to call should robbers or rapists attack them, no cell phones or computers, no mail or fax machines, and no emergency housing sites or food banks. They crossed the Arnon and Jordan rivers, and they ascended mountains and descended into valleys. They may or may not have had donkeys to aid them in their travel. Either way, they were alone on their journey — an unsafe venture for two women.

Jesus' very self is both genetically and culturally diverse, given Ruth's Moabite background, from a people whom the Israelites hated and considered morally depraved.[14] Anger and distrust had flamed on both sides. The Moabites had refused the Israelites bread and water during their long desert trek and, according to the Bible, they had descended from an incestuous liaison of Lot's older daughter with her father. As a result, intermarriage and even the seeking of peace were forbidden (Deuteronomy 23:4-7, Nehemiah 13:1-3, 23-25). Ruth gives a genetic wholeness to Jesus' makeup as well as a sense of cultural diversity.

Did Boaz and Ruth have intercourse on the threshing room floor? The Bible is unclear on this point, and through the centuries, valid arguments have existed on both sides. After much consideration, this author has come to believe they did not. While Ruth literally put herself at Boaz' feet, he seems to have assumed the role of her protector, much like Joseph did for Mary. Chances are that Boaz would not have put Ruth's honor at risk.

Traits of ancestors often show up in their descendants. Consider these qualities in King David and their possible origin: his musical and lyrical talent and Ruth's eloquent, almost musical words; his unwillingness to flee in the face of enemies and Naomi's unrelenting determination; his fierce determination to protect his people and Boaz' role as protector. The author of many psalms, a musician, and a steadfast protector of his people, King David seems to have inherited these qualities from his unforgettable progenitors.

For Ruth and Naomi's stories: The Book of Ruth (4 chapters)
Ruth's Plea: Ruth 1:15-17

Learn more about *The Song of Songs*

One of the most evocative and stunning pieces of literature in the Bible, *The Song of Songs* is a gift to those who take the time to read and absorb it. More than words or simple longings, the poetry reaches the hidden depths of the heart, revealing a young woman's acute and passionate search for the man she loves. Propelled by the desire to be safely in his arms, she will not rest, and in fact takes a dangerous journey through the streets of

Jerusalem, looking for him. And that is why its inclusion in the Bible is so important. Love, lust and desire are not shamefully hidden away, but rather, celebrated in the context of a rewarding and loving relationship. The Bible would be a lesser document were this story not part of it.

In a time when so many marriages were arranged, and polygamy was common, this epic poem lifts up a woman who is outside the mainstream. Children and/or security are not her goals; love is. Interestingly, she is apparently a woman beyond the first bloom of youth: "I am weathered, but still elegant."

What exactly is the relationship between Shulammite (some scholars say this is where she is from; others say it is her name) and her lover? And who is the "king-lover" to whom she refers? Several possibilities exist: 1) she was engaged to Solomon to be one of his seven hundred wives and the book describes both their courtship and week-long wedding festivities; 2) she is engaged to a shepherd from the north country, has been taken to be one of Solomon's wives and is now searching relentlessly for the man she loves; 3) the book is the combination of several stories handed down through the ages about love and longing. This writer believes that the maiden had come to Jerusalem under duress because she had attracted Solomon's representatives — always apparently searching for the most beautiful of young women for the king — but wishes desperately to be back in the arms of her true love. "It is this [Solomon's] wooing and the Shulammite's refusal, that constitutes the action for the Song," writes author Edith Deen.[15] Perhaps it was the king's guards who beat her (*Song of Songs* 5:7) when she did not willingly enter Solomon's harem.

Who is the author of the text and why is it in the Bible, especially if there is no mention of God? While officially attributed to

Solomon, it seems that there must be a woman's hand involved in the writing of it. Most likely, it is several poems strung together, handed down over the ages. Its inclusion in the Bible is thought by many to celebrate the sacrament of marriage and has, over the centuries, inspired many Christians and Jews to reflect on the ardent love that God has for his people and their deep longing for him. Some Christians have also understood it to be an allegorical representation of the passionate love that Jesus has for his Church.

Whatever the exact meaning, *The Song of Songs* is a celebration of the human heart and body, pulsing like a heartbeat, while describing love on all levels: physical, emotional and spiritual. Says writer Naomi Harris Rosenblatt: "The poem is the outstanding example of the Bible's celebration of human sexuality as an integral, positive aspect of life and God's gift to his children...the Song of Songs is the Bible's most lushly sensual treatment of sexuality..."[16]

The Queen of Sheba remains a mysterious, albeit compelling figure in both the Bible and in the canons of Eastern and Western literature. One story that continues to attract significant interest is this: the queen conceived a son by Solomon, and named him Menelik I. Years later, Menelik returned to Jerusalem and stole the precious Ark of the Covenant, which contained the original stone tablets upon which Moses had inscribed the Ten Commandments. Bringing the ark to the temple at Aksum in Ethiopia, Menelik surrounded himself with a group of Hebrew elders who founded the Ethiopian state. Some swear the ark is still there in Ethiopia, although always under heavy guard. At least for now, the mystery remains just that: a mystery.

Learn more about Mary

What is known about Mary? She is a child-woman from Galilee, engaged to marry a carpenter named Joseph; she is from the genealogical line of King David; she is given a choice whether to bear God's son; and the option she chooses changes the world forever. She marries Joseph, bears other children after Jesus, inspires his first miracle, tracks the somewhat defiant twelve year-old down in Jerusalem, watches him work and is turned away at least once while Jesus ministers to the crowds, then stands at the foot of the cross, watching him die. Her love for him never wavers; she is, in many ways, Jesus' first disciple.

What would have happened if Mary had said no to Jesus' birth? Would the Son of God have been born? Would God have chosen someone else? Had God asked before? This much we know: Jesus would not have been the same without Mary as his mother and God would have found a way to break through to humankind had she deferred or rejected the request. God is not dissuaded or held back due to human failure. Even failings get used, as Paul writes in the letter to the Romans: "We know that all things work together for good for those who love God, who are called according to his purpose." (Romans 8:28)

Did God know Mary would say yes? While God no doubt can foresee the future, the whole concept of free will means that the choice truly was Mary's, and that she was as free to say no as to say yes. As to the question of whether God knew her answer in advance, consider this: if free will is truly free, then God wouldn't have known — at least in linear time. Yet if, as is most likely, God sees beyond the realm of human-based time, then the answer is yes. The truth: God asked, respecting Mary's autonomy.

There were no footnotes in the conversation between Mary and Gabriel. Gabriel did not say he would be back to negotiate further should she be unable to decide. There was no waiting time, no "Call me when you've had a chance to think about it." That is often the way it is with God. Rahab had to make a decision on the spot as the king's men came to her door. War was literally on the horizon when Barak asked Deborah to accompany him to the battlefield. Naomi was leaving for Bethlehem with or without Ruth. Like the decisions faced by the women in this book, choices often come along for the Christian that require a decision on the spot.

An interesting parallel: over a thousand years earlier, Ruth had come on foot with her mother-in-law from Moab to Bethlehem, also under physical duress, hers due to hunger and grief. She found protection with Boaz, just as Mary found it with Joseph. Three generations later, David, who would grow to be Israel's mightiest king, would be born. In that little holy town for generations, all was unfolding under God's direction. No wonder the star shone brightly overhead.

For Mary's story: Luke 1:26-45, 2:1-21, 33-51; John 19:25b-27
Mary's Song (The Magnificat) Luke 1:46-56

Learn more about Well Woman

Throughout the ages, this story has captivated readers, and it is the longest recorded conversation that Jesus has with anyone, male or female. Ironically, the name of the woman is unknown.

Why was it such an event for Jesus to speak to a woman? Boundaries were much different between men and women in Jesus' time, especially for rabbis, as many understood Jesus to be. As William Barclay points out, "A rabbi might not even speak to his own wife or daughter or sister in public. There were even

Pharisees who were called 'the bruised and bleeding Pharisees because they shut their eyes when they saw a woman on the street and so walked into walls and houses!' For a rabbi to be seen speaking to a woman in public was the end of his reputation – and yet Jesus spoke to this woman...a woman of notorious character."[17]

Imagine the encounter between Jesus and this unnamed woman, outcast by her community because of a series of husbands and a current live-in lover. Through the ages, she has been found consistently "at fault" – after all, why would anyone have five husbands? What was the matter with her? Think again. In the first century, writes J. Ellsworth Kalas (*Strong was her Faith*), a husband could get a divorce for multiple reasons: for example, if his wife spilled a dish of food, if she spoke disrespectfully of her husband's family or for larger causes, the most common of which was infertility.[18]

What brings worth to this woman? Conventional wisdom has said that it was Jesus who gave her value, breaking down cultural boundaries. But what about having value on her own? She was bright, articulate and intellectually curious. If she had lived in the twenty-first century, she might have been a scholar or a lawyer, pressing hard in her quest for knowledge and truth.

What about the man with whom the woman is currently living that is not her husband? Does that relationship skew her moral character further? Kalas (see above) believes not, given that the only options available to unmarried women seemed to be begging or prostitution. "To live with a man unmarried was at least preferable to becoming a woman of the street...when one man put her out, she didn't take her life or sell it out to prostitution; she tried again. And again...There was a tenacious quality in this woman of Samaria."[19]

Yet another example of Jesus interacting with unorthodox characters (consider his interaction with lepers, tax collectors, criminals and the like), this story continues to break down stereotypes of who is acceptable in God's kingdom and who is chosen or inspired to spread the Good News. Again, a wall has been breached – this time with a scorned woman whose reputation is in shreds. Author Rose Sallberg Kam puts it this way: "When God's kingdom breaks into the world, the most despised are welcome, and a messy personal life bars no one from spreading the gospel."[20]

Like tectonic plates about to collide, our twenty-first century world is damaged by religious conflict, but much of American society seems unable to discuss religious differences in public for fear of offending others. This simple conversation between Jesus and the unnamed woman provides a model of how religious discourse might best be approached: frank, open and fully engaged in discussing the meaning of spirituality, historical context and truth.

The enmity between Jews and Samaritans goes back to 720 BC, when northern Israel, with its capital at Samaria, fell to the Assyrians. Many Jews were carried off in captivity, and foreigners were brought in to resettle the land. Almost immediately, marriages occurred between the remaining Jews and the foreigners. This mixed race, called the Samaritans, inflamed the Jews of Jesus' time, because they believed that God had called them to marry only among themselves. Bitter antagonism between the two sides was the result.

For Well Woman's story: John 4:4-29

Learn more about Martha of Bethany

Questions abound about this story: Why did Jesus wait for two days until starting out for Bethany once he heard that Lazarus was terribly ill? And then, knowing that Lazarus was dead, did Jesus linger for the sole purpose of convincing the disciples that he was the Messiah through the raising of Lazarus? Could he see Lazarus beyond the grave? Why did he wait for Mary to begin crying if he knew he was going to raise Lazarus, as is implied? Perhaps there were more people to heal on the road before he turned toward Bethany, more relationships to forge, more of God's work to declare. Like God, Jesus was working on his own unhurried time, confident that, in the words of Julian of Norwich, "All shall be well and all shall be well and all manner of thing [sic] shall be well."

Practical, forthright, and unapologetic, Martha stood firm, uttering the thought that had no doubt burned into her heart in the days since Lazarus' death: "Lord, if you had been here, my brother would not have died." Such words say much about Martha as they do Jesus. Confident and realistic, she is directing her thoughts at him with whom she can share her deepest self without fear of rejection or diminishment. The bottom line: Full healing is unlikely to be found unless the heart is emptied first into the hands of the One who created it.

Through her drive to seek out Jesus, Martha finds herself in a key conversation with him about his identity that is paralleled by only one other conversation in the Bible, between Jesus and Simon Peter, the "rock" of the early church. Jesus tells Martha, "I am the resurrection and the life." Martha responds with a climactic statement: "You are the Messiah, the Son of God, who has come into the world." (John 11:27)

Martha of Bethany, known for her gracious hospitality, must

have made her guests feel quite comfortable if Jesus and the disciples kept returning. No doubt food was plentiful and tasty, seasoned with fresh herbs. Linens were clean and fresh. Guests settled back for laughter and for a relaxed time.

Martha has been the subject of condescension over the centuries, likened to women who only worry about details, never taking time for themselves. Jesus, during another visit, praised Mary, her sister, for "having the better part," when Martha complained that Mary was not helping her enough in the kitchen. Jesus, however, would not have enjoyed coming to the little Bethany home had not Martha been such a hard worker, tending carefully to the needs of her guests. She deserves to be recognized in our time for her gifts, character and exceptional relationship with Jesus.

In Ezekiel 37, there is a famous scene of God's breathing life into the valley of dry bones, symbolizing the spiritual and physical restoration of the Jewish people during captivity by the Babylonians: "...suddenly there was a noise, a rattling, and the bones came together, bone to its bone...the breath came into them, and they lived, and stood on their feet, a vast multitude." Take a minute and fully imagine Lazarus, staggering into the sunlight, truly raised from the dead — dry bones, indeed!

Ancient legend has it that Martha went on to become a missionary, and traveled as far as what is now modern-day France, performing such deeds as taming a dragon with holy water in her quest to spread the word about Jesus and protect his people. As stated by Elisabeth Moltmann-Wendel, Martha overcame a dragon — "a dragon who was the embodiment of evil, the demonic and the old order. In the Middle Ages she was often painted as the proud housewife, with a fettered dragon stretched out at her feet."[21] For those who are skeptical, try this:

There is no one better suited in the New Testament for such a mission than Martha, given her single-mindedness, strength, and rock solid conviction of faith after witnessing Jesus raise her brother from the dead.

For Martha of Bethany's story: John 11:1-44 (also Luke 10:38-42)

Learn more about Mary of Bethany

Given that walking was the main mode of transportation in Jesus' time, and guests usually arrived with dusty and dirty feet, foot-washing was a common gesture meant to welcome the tired traveler. Anointing with oil was also a known symbol, as kings such as Saul and David had been anointed as a sign of royalty, and bodies were anointed with fragrant spices as part of preparing them before burial. By her action, Mary accomplished three things: she welcomed Jesus, she acknowledged his kingship, and she began the process of preparing him for death.

Mary and Jesus met on a soul level. What if he had never been anointed? Although his steps toward the cross would have been the same, perhaps he had more courage in his heart, more peace in his soul. On one of Jesus' previous visits, Mary had irked her sister, Martha, because she did not prepare dinner but rather sat at Jesus' feet, taking in all he had to say. On a more recent occasion, Jesus had raised her brother, Lazarus, from the grave, only after Mary shared her grief, causing him to weep as well. Given her particular gift of living in the moment, it makes sense that she is the one now to breathe deeply and reach out to Jesus in a way that fed both their souls.

Extravagance is the keyword in this story. Mary was extravagant in her gift of fragrant oil — the scent of which filled the entire house — and with her very self, wiping Jesus' feet with her hair.

As J. Ellsworth Kalas writes, the act was not isolated from Mary's person. "Mary was entirely in character at this moment. She was an extravagant personality, and she had found the person who merited extravagance such as hers."[22]

Mary's actions are clearly sensual. A heavily-scented and precious oil, John describes the "scent of the perfume as filling the entire house." Wiping Jesus' feet with her hair was a particularly feminine action, one that must have made a clear impression on those who watched, as the story is reported in all four Gospels. Women simply did not touch men in this way. Footwashing would usually have been done by a male, the head of the house, when the guest arrived, not after dinner and conversation. The disciples grew angry, expressing their frustration over the cost of the nard and how the money could better be given to the poor. That anger may have been sparked by their unease with Mary's act itself.

The angry reaction of the disciples is also consistent throughout the Gospels. Given that a jar of nard cost the equivalent of one year's salary — which, at minimum wage would mean more than $10,000 in modern day currency — Judas leads the argument. Jesus comes to Mary's rescue, asking the disciples to honor him, understanding that she is preparing him for his last days. Ironically, immediately after this event, Judas leaves and betrays Jesus for thirty pieces of sliver.

Although the story of a woman anointing Jesus' feet with oil occurs in all the Gospels, only John's account names Mary of Bethany as the one to have performed the act, and that is the version followed in the story above.

For Mary of Bethany's story: John 12:1-8 (also Luke 10:38-42)

Learn more about Mary Magdalene

Many in the church, including various authors, artists and theologians, have portrayed Mary Magdalene as a prostitute before she met Jesus. There has also been the lingering story, popular in some recent books and movies such as The Da Vinci Code, that she was sexually involved with Jesus and bore his children. No basis exists in the Gospels to authenticate these claims; rather, what is reported is that Jesus cast out seven demons from her. In biblical times, demons were understood to be spirits that would inhabit a person's body, taking over actions and words. Today, her condition would most likely be understood as mental illness.

Essential to understanding her story – and what all four Gospels portray – is this: Mary Magdalene is a bold, expressive woman who loves Jesus deeply, for she has experienced life-changing healing at the hands of her friend and Lord. "More than a mere disciple or servant," says author Scott Spencer, "Mary has effectively been called, as were the disciples in the upper room, Jesus' friend."[23] And what a friend she was. For centuries, Christians have noted that Mary Magdalene was the first to see the risen Jesus, the first to be called by name by the risen Lord, the first to proclaim the resurrection. Magdalene (who gets her name because she is from the town of Magdala) was front and center as God's greatest story unfolded, not cast to the side because of her gender or her history.

Did Jesus know that it would be Mary Magdalene that came looking for him after his death? Had he missed her and the others during his three-day descent to the dead? Did he long to tarry with her, to tell his friends about what he had seen in that time? What had he seen? Legend has it that he was freeing souls from Satan's embrace. This much is certain: Jesus was changed, endowed with the certainty of life after death. To Mary's chagrin, however, he was not able to embrace her or even linger with those who had become his closest friends.

Why exactly did Mary and the other women go to Jesus' tomb? The details between the different Gospels vary. In John's retelling, it is a custom to visit the grave of a loved one, especially three days after death. In Luke, they take spices to anoint the body, which would have been forbidden on the evening of the Sabbath and the Sabbath day itself. The main denominator is this: they loved Jesus deeply, and went to the place where they believed his body to be, trying to be as close to him as possible. Little did they know the joy that awaited them.

For Mary Magdalene's story: John 20:1-18; Luke 8:1-3

Endnotes

1 As the Bible is primarily oral tradition from a number of sources, dates cannot fully be known. However, for clarity of purpose here, chronological estimates are taken from Thomas Robinson, *The Bible Timeline* (Barnes and Noble, 2000).

2 Theory (partial) attributed to Francine Rivers, *Unashamed: Rahab, The Lineage of Grace Series*, (Carol Stream, Illinois: Tyndale House Publishers, 2001).

3 Edith Deen, *All the Women of the Bible*, (New York: Harper and Row, 1955) page 65.

4 Tikva Frymer-Kensky, *Reading the Women of the Bible*, (New York, New York: Schocken Books, 2002) page 40.

5 Irene Nowell, *Women in the Old Testament*, (Collegeville, Minnesota: The Liturgical Press, 1997) page 62.

6 Miki Raver, *Listen to Her Voice:* Women of the Hebrew Bible, (San Francisco, California: Chronicle Books, 1998) page 25.

7 Smithsonian Magazine, Volume 18, No. 2, May 1987.

8 Irene Nowell, *Women in the Old Testament*, page 14.

9 Irene Nowell, *Women in the Old Testament*, page 16.

10 Joseph Telushkin, *Biblical Literacy: The Most Important People, Places, and Events of the Hebrew Bible*, (New York: William Morrow and Company, New York) page 169.

11 Tikva Frymer-Kensky, *Reading the Women of the Bible*, page 53.

12 Irene Nowell, *Women in the Old Testament*, page 269.

13 Richard Bauckham, *Gospel Women: Studies of the Named Women in the Gospels*, (Grand Rapids, Michigan/ Cambridge: William B. Eerdmans Publishing Company, 2002) pages 62-63.

14 Miki Raver, *Listen to Her Voice: Women of the Hebrew Bible*, page 149.

15 Edith Deen, *All the Women of the Bible*, page 366.

16 Naomi Harris Rosenblatt, *After the Apple: Women in the Bible — Timeless Stories of Love, Lust and Longing*, (New York: Miramax Books, 2005) page 246.

17 William Barclay, *The Gospel of John*, Volume 1, (Philadelphia, Pennsylvania: Westminster Press, 1975) page 151.

18 J. Ellsworth Kalas, *Strong was her Faith: Women of the New Testament*, (Nashville, Tennessee: Abingdon Press, 2007) page 54.

19 J. Ellsworth Kalas, *Strong was Her Faith*, page 55.

20 Rose Sallberg Kam, *Their Stories, Our Stories: Women of the Bible*, (New York, New York: Continuum International Publishing Group, 1995) page 214.

21 Elisabeth Moltmann-Wendel, *The Women Around Jesus*, (NY, New York: The Crossroad Publishing Company, 1982) page 27.

22 J. Ellsworth Kalas, *Strong was her Faith: Women of the New Testament*, page 38.

23 F. Scott Spencer, *Dancing Girls, Loose Ladies, and Women of the Cloth*, (New York, New York: The Continuum Publishing Group, 2004) page 98.

Sources and Further Reading

Barclay, William, *The Gospel of John,* Volume I, Philadelphia, Pennsylvania: The Westminster Press, 1975.

Bauckham, Richard, *Gospel Women: Studies of the Named Women in the Gospels,* Grand Rapids, Michigan: William B. Eerdmans Publishing Company, 2002.

Bellis, Alice Ogden, *Helpmates, Harlots, Heroes, Women's Stories in the Hebrew Bible,* Louisville, Kentucky: Westminster/John Knox Press, 1994.

Brueggemann, Walter, *The Land: Place as Gift, Promise and Challenge in Biblical Faith,* Minneapolis, Minnesota: Fortress Press, Minneapolis, 2002.

Chiffolo, Anthony F., and Hesse, Rayner, W., Jr., *Cooking with the Bible: Biblical Food, Feasts, and Lore,* Greenwood Press, Westport, Connecticut, 2006.

Chittister, Joan, *The Friendship of Women, The Hidden Tradition of the Bible,* NY, New York: Bluebridge, 2006.

Davis, Ellen F., *Who Are You, My Daughter? Reading Ruth Through Image and Text,* Louisville: Westminster John Knox Press, 2003.

Deen, Edith, *All of the Women of the Bible,* San Francisco: Harper and Row, 1955.

Essex, Barbara J., *More Bad Girls of the Bible,* Cleveland, Ohio: The Pilgrim Press, 2009.

Frymer-Kensky, Tikva, *Reading the Women of the Bible: A New Interpretation of their Stories,* New York, NY: Schocken Books, 2002.

Getty-Sullivan, Mary Ann, *Women in the New Testament,* Collegeville, Minnesota: The Liturgical Press, 2001.

Higgs, Liz Curtis, *Bad Girls of the Bible and What We Can Learn From Them,* Colorado Springs, Colorado: WaterBrook Press, 1999.

Kalas, J. Ellsworth, *Strong was her Faith: Women of the New Testament*, Nashville, Tennessee: Abingdon Press, 2007.

Kam, Rose Sallberg, *Their Stories, Our Stories*, New York, NY: Continuum, New York, 1995.

Klein, Lillian R., *From Deborah to Esther, Sexual Politics in the Hebrew Bible*, Minneapolis, Minnesota: Fortress Press, 2003.

Nowell, Irene, *Women in the Old Testament*, Collegeville, Minnesota: The Liturgical Press, 1997.

Metzger, Bruce M., and Coogan, Michael D., *The Oxford Guide to People and Places of the Bible*, New York, NY: Oxford University Press, 2001.

McKenna, Megan, *Leave Her Alone*, New York, NY: Orbis Books, 2000.

Mirkin, Marsha, *The Women Who Danced by the Sea: Finding Ourselves in the Stories of our Biblical Foremothers*, Rhinebeck, New York: Monkfish Book Publishing Company, 2004.

Ochs, Vanessa L., *Sarah Laughed, Modern Lessons from the Wisdom and Stories of Biblical Women*, McGraw-Hill, 2004.

Odelain, O. and Séguineau, R., *Dictionary of Proper Names and Places in the Bible*, Garden City, New York: Doubleday and Company, 1981.

Moltmann-Wendel, Elisabeth, *The Women Around Jesus*, NY, New York: The Crossroad Publishing Company, 1982.

Raver, Miki, *Women of the Hebrew Bible*, San Francisco, California: Chronicle Books, 1998.

Rosenblatt, Naomi Harris, *After the Apple: Women in the Bible — Timeless Stories of Love, Lust, and Longing*, New York, NY: Miramax Books, 2005.

Ritley, M.R., *God of Our Mothers: Face to Face with the Powerful Women of the Old Testament*, Harrisburg, Pennsylvania: Morehouse Publishing, 2006.

Spencer, F. Scott, *Dancing Girls, Loose Ladies, and Women of the Cloth*, New York, New York: The Continuum Publishing Group, 2004.

Spina, Frank Anthony, *The Faith of the Outsider, Exclusion and Inclusion in the Biblical Story,* Grand Rapids, Michigan, William B. Eerdmans Publishing Company, 2005.

Soelle, Dorothee and Kirchberger, Joe H., *Great Women of the Bible in Art and Literature,* Minneapolis, Minnesota: Fortress Press, 2006.

Telushkin, Joseph, Biblical Literacy: *The Most Important People, Events and Ideas of the Hebrew Bible,* New York, NY: William Morrow and Company, 1997.

Acknowledgments

In the five years it took to research, write and produce this book, many people helped through their expertise, knowledge, enthusiasm and support.

The following authors and books were especially helpful: Edith Deen, *All the Women of the Bible*; Francine Rivers for her novella series on Rahab, Tamar, Ruth, Bathsheba and Mary; Naomi Harris Rosenblatt for *After the Apple: Women in the Bible — Timeless Stories of Love, Lust and Longing*; Miki Raver for *Listen to Her Voice: Women of the Hebrew Bible*; and Liz Curtis Higgs for her *Bad Girls of the Bible series*.

Invaluable in offering their support and enthusiasm were the following colleagues: The Rev. Noel Bailey; Carol Barnwell; Sarah Bartenstein; Barbara Braver; Cindy Hilger; Mark J. Duffy; The Rev. Roger Ezell; Roxanne Ezell; Barbara Forster; Karen Greenfeld; Pamela Grossman; The Rt. Rev. James L. Jelinek; Donald Kraus; The Rev. Dr. Sheryl A. Kujawa-Holbrook; The Rev. Loren B. Mead; The Rev. Anne Miner-Pearson; Cindy Piper; The Rev. Mary Frances Schjonberg; The Rev. Louis (Skip) Shuedding; The Rev. Dr. Richard H. Schmidt; The Very Rev. Spenser D. Simrill; The Rev. A. Wayne Schwab; The Rev. Peggy Tuttle; The Rev. Canon Jean Parker Vail; and Georgia Wiester. Also key were the librarians and staff of St. Paul's Luther Seminary, in whose book stacks I spent many long and happy hours.

I am grateful as well for the exceptional talent of the artist, Karen N. Canton. Her paintings are brilliant. She visually brought to life women who would have been one dimensional without her talent and commitment to this project. Blending components of both medieval and contemporary art, she has woven together deep and playful tapestries that both complement and complete the book. Eric Canton, her husband, has also been of enormous help, working many hours to handle a wide range of literary and technological aspects of this endeavor.

Many thanks to O Books and John Hunt, publisher, and to agent Krista Goering of the Krista Goering Literary Agency, LLC. Publishing is a rapidly evolving venture and they are inspiring and hope-filled guides in what has seemed like a wilderness at times.

Finally, I am deeply appreciative and take great joy in the writing partnership I have with my husband of twenty years, the Rev. Leonard Freeman. This book would be a much lesser product without his companionship, wit, and deep well of creative energy. With his help, the women in these pages have turned into real people — alive, discerning, spirited, passionate, dynamic individuals, just like God calls all of us to be.

LHF

An Expression of Thanks

I want to thank the Rev. Lindsay Hardin Freeman, the wise and creative author of this book, who believed in me and my art. Also enormous gratitude goes out to my daughter Greta who corrected my work with her insights and my daughter Anna, my best cheerleader, and last but not least, my poodle Emily who sat for hours at my feet in patient devotion.

KNC